WORKING WITH TILE

By the Editors of Sunset Books

Sunset Books
President and VP Sales: Richard A. Smeby
Production Director: Lory Day
Editorial Director: Bob Doyle
Art Director: Vasken Guiragossian

Working With Tile was produced with the assistance of
St. Remy Press
President: Pierre Léveillé
Managing Editor: Carolyn Jackson
Senior Editor: Heather Mills
Senior Art Director: Francine Lemieux

Book Consultants
William Sturrock
Don Vandervort

Special Contributors
Eric Beaulieu, Michel Blais, Normand Boudreault,
Jean-Pierre Bourgeois, Caroline Bowden, Robert Chartier,
François Daxhelet, Hélène Dion, Jean-Guy Doiron,
Lorraine Doré, Dominique Gagné, Michel Giguère,
Christine M. Jacobs, Solange Laberge, Alfred LeMaitre,
François Longpré, Geneviève Monette, Jennifer Ormston,
Jacques Perrault, Rebecca Smollett, Michelle Turbide,
Adam van Sertima, Natalie Watanabe, Judy Yelon

COVER: Tile courtesy of ANN SACKS Tile & Stone. Cover
design by Susan Bryant. Photography by Philip Harvey.
Photo direction and styling by JoAnn Masaoka Van Atta.

Acknowledgments
Thanks to the following:
American Olean Tile Company, Lansdale, PA
APA-The Engineered Wood Association, Tacoma, WA
Argosy Importers and Distributors Ltd., Edmonton, Alta.
Armstrong World Industries Inc., Lancaster, PA and
    Montreal, Que.
Burke Industries, San Jose, CA
Michael Byrne, Grand Isle, VT
Ceratec Inc., Ville St. Laurent, Que.
Congoleum Corporation, Mercerville, NJ
Crossville Ceramics, Crossville, TN
DAL-TILE, Concord, Ont.
Richard Day, Palomar Mountain, CA
Endicott Clay Products Co., Fairbury, NE
Harris-Tarkett Inc., Johnson City, TN
Hartco Flooring Company, Knoxville, TN
W.W. Henry Co., Huntington Park, CA
Kentucky WoodFloors Inc., Louisville, KY
Laticrete International, Aurora, Ont. and Bethany, CT
Giles Miller-Mead, Brome, Que.
National Oak Flooring Manufacturers Association,
    Memphis, TN
National Wood Flooring Association, Manchester, MO
Peace Flooring Company Inc., Magnolia, AR
Resilient Floor Covering Institute, Rockville, MD
State of Vermont Agency of Natural Resources,
    Waterbury, VT
State of Vermont Department of Health, Burlington, VT
Stern and Associates, Cranford, NJ
Terrazzo, Tile, and Marble Association of Canada,
    Concord, Ont.
Tile Council of America, Clemson, SC

Picture Credits
p. 4   courtesy American Olean Tile Co.
p. 5   Steve Marley
p. 6   *(upper)* courtesy American Olean Tile Co.
p. 6   *(lower)* Steve Marley
p. 7   *(upper)* courtesy American Olean Tile Co.
p. 7   *(lower)* Steve Marley
p. 8   *(both)* courtesy American Olean Tile Co.
p. 9   *(upper)* Steve Marley
p. 9   *(lower)* courtesy American Olean Tile Co.
p. 10 courtesy Armstrong World Industries Inc.
p. 11 *(upper)* courtesy Congoleum Corporation
p. 11 *(lower)* courtesy Armstrong World Industries Inc.
p. 12 *(upper)* courtesy Armstrong World Industries Inc.
p. 12 *(lower)* Steve Marley
p. 13 Steve Marley
p. 14 *(both)* courtesy Kentucky WoodFloors Inc.
p. 15 *(upper)* courtesy Kentucky WoodFloors Inc.
p. 15 *(lower)* courtesy Harris-Tarkett Inc.
p. 16 courtesy American Olean Tile Co.

CONTENTS

TILING POSSIBILITIES

The way in which tile adapts itself to every style and taste is sheer magic; you can match any mood, create any kind of appearance. After you've chosen between ceramic, resilient vinyl, or wood (also known as parquet), there are choices to be made among the hundreds, even thousands, of designs, textures, sizes, shapes, and colors that are available to create the effect you've been dreaming about.

Tile can be used in almost any room in the house. In addition to using tile on your floors and walls, you can experiment with ceramic tiles on countertops, or as trim around fireplaces. Brighten your kitchen by using hand-painted ceramic tiles on the backsplashes or on the kickplates below the lower cabinets. Ceramic tile can also be laid outdoors *(page 60)*. The photographs on the following pages will show how you can be inventive with tiling, even in the most practical of applications.

No matter which type of tile you choose or where you plan to install it, successful results require careful planning and meticulous preparation. Separate chapters on ceramic tile, resilient tile, and parquet (wood tile) give you information on the selection of tile and the preparation of the backing—the surface that supports the tile—prior to the actual installation, as well as detailed installation instructions. The chapter on outdoor paving includes ceramic tile as well as other paving materials. We'll also give you guidelines on maintaining your tile floor and how to make repairs.

This bathroom makes excellent use of ceramic tile to create a look that is both practical and simple.

CERAMIC TILE

The designs and textures that are available in today's commercial ceramic tile almost always guarantee impressive results. Manufacturers often provide a single type of tile in a wide range of colors, allowing you to select a small group of colors for a graphic design or a monochromatic theme. Another method to consider is using tile seconds, which are usually sold at a low price; any defects are usually quirks in appearance rather than deformities in the tiles themselves.

A decorative tile entryway gives a home a welcoming feel. You can choose anything from a complex overall pattern to something simple yet elegant. In the kitchen, ceramic tile has a myriad of uses on countertops, backsplashes, or kickplates, as well as on floors and walls. In the bathroom, tile can create an innovative look, fresh from the pages of today's interior design magazines. As well as being installed on the floor or in the bathtub enclosure, ceramic tile works well to liven up the counter around a washbasin.

At the heart of many homes is the fireplace. Although originally intended as a functional heating device, a fireplace can be a decorative focal point as well. Tile is an ideal material for fireplace use because it is impervious to heat and easy to clean.

Although ceramic tiles appear predominantly in interior settings, don't forget that their attractive permanence makes them ideal for outdoor use as well. Entry steps, walkways, and patios are some common applications, and you'll find that the results enhance the exterior of any home.

Quarry tile—large, uniform, and undecorated—is a popular way to use ceramic tile to cover the floors of an entire home. Usually available in natural clay colors, quarry tiles range from a raw, earthy appearance to the sophisticated look of the glazed type.

For easy maintenance, ceramic tile is an excellent choice; most types wash clean with mild detergent or an all-purpose household cleaner.

The tremendous versatility of tile is demonstrated here: The same tiles that cover the dining area march right out onto the patio—and are used to line countertops and walls as well. The soft Mexican Saltillo tiles used here give a rustic look. Architect: Batey & Mack, Architects.

Unglazed quarry tile gives this solarium a warm feel. The unglazed surface is also more slip-resistant than glazed tile. The tile can be used both indoors, as shown here, or outdoors on the patio or at poolside.

Framing this old-fashioned fireplace with a row of blue and white tiles reinforces its simple and dignified lines, although the scroll-like design of these hand-painted Portuguese tiles introduces richness and complexity. The quarry tiles used for the hearth have been stained to blend with the wood on the floor, and then sealed. Architect: J. Allen Sayles, Architectural Kitchens and Baths.

Ceramic tile is used for both practical and decorative purposes in this kitchen. Tile on the countertop and backsplash make spills easy to clean up. The mixture of white and blue tile creates a bright and airy cooking space.

Narrow and curved "bead" tile pieces offer an attractive alternative for a bathroom basin trim. Cutting tiles to fit is a difficult and time-consuming task, but the end result is spectacular.
Design: Tile by Buzz.

By mixing and matching colors, you can design an inviting setting for a relaxing soak in the bath. The versatility of ceramic tile encourages you to be creative.

This vanity area employs tile on every available surface. In addition, colorful design strips accent tile on walls and counters to create a subtle atmosphere of elegance and delicacy. A little knowledge and skill can make your design ideas as limitless as your imagination.

Outdoors, sand-colored quarry tiles transform plain concrete slabs into an inviting entry. Each square tile is surrounded by lozenge-shaped "pickets" to create an overall octagonal pattern. Design: Designed Environ, Inc.

Re-creating the look of classical times, these ceramic tiles have the look of granite, but not the price. In the foyer, the mixture of plain and mosaic-inspired tile gives visitors a sophisticated welcome.

RESILIENT TILE

Resilient tile is an extremely versatile alternative to ceramic tile. As with ceramics, resilient tile comes in standard sizes and shapes that are easy to apply.

Resilient tile is laid either with adhesive or with self-stick material on the tile back. It comes in a wide variety of colors and designs, from plain tile to discreet, traditional patterns and the latest matchings of color and motif. Resilient tile can also take on any number of appearances, from brick to slate, marble, wood, and even ceramic. All that you need to do is decide which design best suits your individual taste and the mood you're trying to create. From there, it's a simple matter to install the tiles, and you'll soon be enjoying your new resilient tile floor.

Resilient tile is losing its staid image, as shown in this bright, lively bathroom. The nonabsorbent surface of this type of tile means that water can be mopped up easily with no worries about staining.

Increasingly, resilient tile is coming out of the kitchen and into the front hall. Today's new designs are refined and versatile enough for any room in the house.

This kitchen exudes a fresh, springlike appeal thanks to the bright simplicity of the green and white tile.

Resilient tile can be made to look like other materials. These tiles, for instance, have a marble design which adds a certain degree of elegance to this bathroom setting.

Another example of the versatility of resilient tile is found in this room—the classic mood owes much to a carefully selected floor covering of white, slate-textured resilient tiles.

PARQUET

A wood floor projects an undeniable sense of warmth and charm. Once only enjoyed by the wealthy, wood tile, or parquet, is now an affordable alternative to both ceramic and resilient tile, and just as easy to install. An aura of permanence and well-bred style surrounds this wood product, for it adds a feeling of old-world quality and history to practically any room environment.

Parquet comes in a variety of designs. Some, like Monticello, are traditional, while others incorporate old patterns into new and innovative designs particular to the manufacturer. Many types of wood can be used in the making of parquet, from the more traditional cherry, walnut, ash, oak, and maple, to exotic teak. The end result is a long-lasting, beautiful expression of nature's work at its finest.

Placing fingerblock parquet tiles in parallel rows, rather than in the more common checkerboard pattern, visually expands this living area. Architect: John Brooks Boyd.

This oak parquet floor has been given a white finish, which lends an unusual but nevertheless sophisticated appearance.

This Mayan walnut parquet, laid out in block pattern, is warm and welcoming.

Mayan cherry parquet adds an air of refined antiquity to this dining room.

Natural white oak parquet in the traditional Monticello pattern brightens a living room.

OTHER TILE MATERIALS

In addition to the popular tiles—ceramic, resilient, and wood—covered in this book, you'll also find a range of tiles made from other materials. Perhaps one of the kinds discussed below will be just right for your remodeling job.

Mirror tiles, usually 12 inches square, come with a wide variety of surface designs. Applied to a wall, they add depth and light to any room. They are affixed to a surface with double-faced mounting tape.

Marble tiles, precut to various sizes, may be used in the same ways as ceramic tile. For decades, marble tiles were considered a hallmark of opulence, but now they cost about the same as high-quality ceramic tiles or hardwood flooring. Installation is similar to that for ceramic tile.

Slate tiles are bluish-black, green, or maroon in color, with either a smooth or—more often—a textured surface. Slate floors are durable and restful to the eyes. They can be installed in the same way as ceramic tiles.

Terrazzo tile is manufactured by setting chips of marble or onyx in concrete and then polishing the surface. Although commonly made in large slabs, terrazzo is also available in 12-inch tiles that can be installed by the homeowner.

For the environmentally conscious do-it-yourselfer, there are now tiles on the market which contain recycled glass. They are intended for heavy-traffic areas. However, these tiles may be hard to find.

Marble tile in your foyer announces to the visitor that this is a home of distinction.

CERAMIC TILE INDOORS

Ceramic tile is one of the oldest, most successful surfacing materials. Brilliantly colored ceramic tiles still beautify the floors, walls, and ceilings of cathedrals, temples, and palaces built many centuries ago. Whether you're building a new home or remodeling an older one, you'll find few surfacing materials that match the decorative impact, versatility, and permanence of ceramic tile. In addition to the pleasure that the finished job will give you, the beauty and durability of ceramic tile will add value to your home.

In this chapter, we'll give you simple instructions on how to choose your materials and tools *(page 18)*; prepare the wall or floor that you're going to tile *(page 31)*; install the tiles *(page 34)*; and finish your project *(page 53)*. The instructions are designed to give a professional look to your project, and a tiled surface that will last for many years. Keep in mind that a tiling project can cause considerable disruption, particularly in a high-traffic area; you should plan out your steps carefully.

The key to a professional-looking tiling job is straight rows. The simplest technique is to butt the first row of tiles against a wood batten fastened to the old floor. Use small pieces of wood, as shown above, to maintain equal spacing between the tiles.

MATERIALS

Ceramic tiles are essentially flat pieces of hard-baked clay. Tiles provide a surface that's fireproof, durable, soil- and moisture-resistant, and easy to maintain. A tiled surface is made up of a group of tiles, each fastened with an adhesive to a subsurface, or backing, and usually bonded to neighboring tiles with a filler material called grout.

Ceramic tile comes in a great variety of colors, patterns, and textures. In choosing tiles, you should consider how you will use the tiled surface and where it will be installed. Will the surface be primarily decorative or must it withstand a steady stream of traffic? Do you want to brighten a dark room or add a subdued, rustic mood to a light study? If the family bathroom is the site, you'll have different requirements than you would for the entry hall. In this section, we'll help you choose the type of tile that is best suited for your use, as well as the right adhesive and grout.

WHERE TO USE CERAMIC TILE

At one time, the use of ceramic tile in the home was restricted to bathrooms and an occasional foyer. Around the turn of the century, however, ceramic tile became popular for almost any room in the house. Today, as described below, ceramic tile is found on both floors and walls in all parts of the house. In the first chapter, you'll see examples of a variety of uses.

Floors: Ceramic tile is a natural for floors. In entryways, halls, and other heavy-traffic corridors, ceramic floor tiles remain rigid and colorfast. An onslaught of wet galoshes or the innocent tracking of a muddy family pet will do no harm to the floor. In the kitchen or bathroom, ceramic tile provides excellent protection against drips and spills; cleaning requires only a damp sponge or cloth.

Tiled flooring adds a strong decorative accent. Depending on the type of tile, you can create any atmosphere —from elegance to rustic informality. Brighten a dark room or make a room appear larger, as shown on the opposite page, by extending the tile floor onto the patio or deck.

Walls: Any wall that might be sprayed or splashed with water is an obvious candidate for ceramic tile. But don't limit tile to areas that get wet. A wall of ceramic tile in a living room, dining room, or den adds a dramatic backdrop for furnishings, plants, or a freestanding fireplace. If the floor is also tiled, choose wall tiles that will complement it.

Tubs and showers: Around tubs and showers, tile provides a waterproof surface that is easy to keep clean of water spots and soap film.

Countertops: Ideal as a working surface around the kitchen sink and stove top, ceramic tile is unaffected by a sharp knife edge or hot pan. If you use a stain-resistant grout, grease and food spots wipe off easily. Tile adds a functional, decorative surface to a bathroom vanity, an eating counter, or a wet bar. Adding a new ceramic tile top will give new life to an old table; tile also adds flair to exposed storage shelves.

Fireplaces: Because they are baked at high temperatures, most ceramic tiles are not affected by heat. Consider using tiles to line the outside face of a fireplace. Even a single row will brighten a room.

Stairs and steps: Constant traffic wears down the treads of stairs and steps. Covering them with tiles will add years of life. For steps, use tiles with a slip-resistant textured finish. And for a simple brightening effect, tile the risers to make the steps more distinctive and visible in dim light.

Decorative borders: Whether they are set edge-to-edge or spaced apart, ceramic tiles provide a beautiful accent border for a door or window. If fastened to the surface and left raised, they may require the addition of a wood or metal border trim. In new construction, it is a relatively simple matter to set border or trim tiles right into the plaster or stucco so the tile faces are flush with the finished wall.

ASK A PRO

HOW CAN I ADD INTEREST TO MY TILING PATTERN?

Consider rimming the edge of a room with contrasting tiles, or working small, colorful tiles into your tiling pattern. If you want to get more elaborate, you can purchase tiles that are designed to be laid in patterns that imitate a rug or quilt. The tiles necessary for entire murals can also be purchased—your dealer will likely have certain ones available, but may also be able to help you design your own.

You can use tile colors, patterns, and designs to alter or control the apparent space in a room. To put these illusions to work for you, here are a few tips:

• A repeated tile pattern that runs lengthwise adds depth to a room *(below, top left)*; running across, it gives a shorter, wider look *(below, bottom left)*.

• To achieve visual unity, continue the same flooring from one room to the next or out onto an exterior patio area *(below, right)*; this also gives a sense of spaciousness.

• A busy tile pattern or mix of several colors makes an area look smaller; using a simple pattern or a single color has the opposite effect.

• Small tiles seem to expand the size of the tiled surface. Large tiles decrease the apparent size of the area.

• Dark colors tend to shrink a given space, while light or bright colors impart an airy, spacious feeling.

• Divide the space within a room into specific activity areas using contrasting tile colors or patterns on the floors.

TYPES OF TILE

Tiles are available in a number of types, depending on how they are made and on their intended use. A key factor to consider in choosing a tile is how easily it absorbs water. Porcelain is the most vitreous (glasslike) and the most water-resistant tile. Nonvitreous, or soft-bodied, tiles readily absorb water; treatment with a sealant makes them water-resistant only to a degree.

Tile can be either glazed or unglazed. A glaze is a hard finish, usually including a color, that is applied to the surface of the clay body (the bisque) before the final baking. Glazes can have a high gloss, a satinlike matte, a semimatte, or a dull, pebbly textured surface. Unglazed tiles do not have a baked-on finish. The colors that you see—commonly earth tones, ranging from yellow to dark red—are either the natural clay color or pigments added prior to forming and baking. This color is consistent throughout the body of the tile.

Handpainted tiles, often created for tile shops by local artists, offer decorative designs such as flowers, trees, and animals. They can be set as individual accents in a backsplash wall or counter. Entire scenes, such as a basket of flowers or a group of swimming whales, can be painted on a group of tiles. Most handpainted tiles are made by professionals, but you can paint your own tiles and have them glazed. Decorative decals can be applied to tiles and make an attractive and cheaper alternative to handpainted tiles. Your dealer can show you decals—again, usually depicting flowers or animals—that are permanently applied to the tiles through a firing process that is done in the store.

Tiles differ in thickness and finish depending on whether they are intended for floors, walls, or counters. Make sure that the type of tile you're buying is appropriate for the surface that you want to cover.

CREATE MARVELS WITH MOSAICS

Ceramic mosaics are among the most colorful and versatile materials in the tile family. Mosaic tiles look striking on floors and walls and the smaller ones can wrap around columns or follow the contours of garden walls and swimming pools.

Whether intended for floors or walls, mosaic tiles are generally small: 3/4 by 3/4 inch on up to 4 by 4 inches. Smaller tiles are mounted on plastic netting or joined together so you can lay out one or two square feet at a time. Shapes include squares, octagons, hexagons, or special designs; some common patterns are shown below.

Mosaics can be of natural clay tile or hard porcelain and are available both glazed and unglazed. Some contain a nonslip additive for safety.

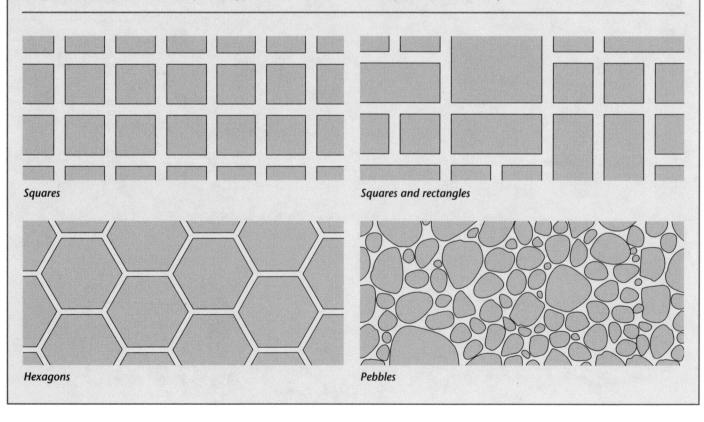

Squares

Squares and rectangles

Hexagons

Pebbles

FLOOR TILES

Compared with wall tiles, floor tiles are generally larger, thicker, and more durable underfoot. Floor tiles come as squares, rectangles, hexagons, and octagons, as well as Moorish, ogee, and other exotic shapes; a selection is shown below.

Floor tiles are available glazed or unglazed; unglazed tiles are less slippery and wear does not show as much because the coloration extends throughout the tile body. Special nonslip tiles are also available.

Quarry tiles: These tiles are made by extruding clay into forms before firing. They come glazed or unglazed in natural clay colors of yellow, brown, or red. Tough and water-resistant (especially when sealed), quarry tile is an ideal flooring surface. Sizes and shapes vary.

Pavers: These tiles are pressed rather than extruded before firing. Pavers are generally unglazed and may need to be sealed to make them water-resistant. These tiles are available in many colors and sizes. A common size is 4 by 8 inches, known as brick pavers. Very dense pavers are called porcelain tiles.

Porcelain tiles: The best porcelain is highly refined clay fired at more than 2000°F to form a dense, hard body. These tiles are often earth-colored, but come in many other colors. They don't need to be sealed.

Glazed tiles: Tiles known as "glazed" are generally made of pressed clay. There are glazed tiles for floors and walls, but wall tiles are often softer and not suitable for floor use. Some glazed floor tiles have textured or matte surfaces for better traction and longer wear.

Button-back tiles, which are often imported from Italy, have a series of small bumps on the underside. These allow the tiles to be stacked in the kiln and still have air space between the individual tiles. Button-back tiles may crack if not bedded properly.

Mexican tiles: These are rustic, earth-colored tiles popular in the Southwest and West. Mexican tiles are soft and highly absorbent, and so need to be sealed.

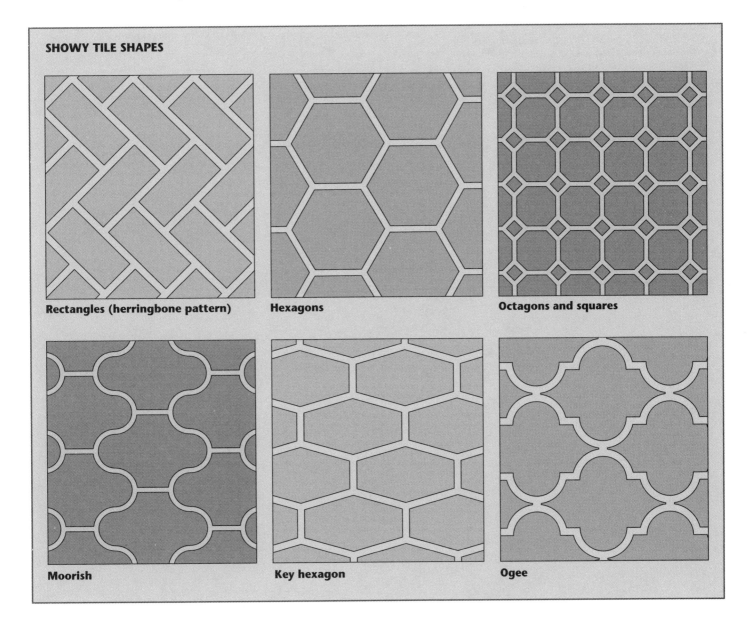

SHOWY TILE SHAPES

Rectangles (herringbone pattern)   Hexagons   Octagons and squares

Moorish   Key hexagon   Ogee

WALL TILES

Tiles that are classified as wall tiles are glazed and offer a tremendous variety of colors and designs. Wall tiles are generally lighter and thinner than floor tiles. Their lightness is a plus for vertical installation. And although the tile bodies are porous, the glazing process makes their surface water-resistant.

Standard sizes for wall tiles range from 3 by 3 inches to $4\frac{1}{4}$ by $8\frac{1}{2}$ inches, with thickness from $\frac{1}{4}$ to $\frac{3}{8}$ inch. Other sizes and shapes are also available.

Many tiles come with specially shaped, matching trim pieces *(below)*. These are designed to finish off edges, form coves, and turn inside and outside corners. Some tiles have matching glazed ceramic accessories— soap dishes, towel bars, and glass and brush holders.

COUNTER TILES

Although primarily intended for covering kitchen and bath countertops, counter tiles can also be used on shelves, windowsills, and tabletops, or as decorative inserts in tables.

Like wall tiles, counter tiles are available in an almost limitless variety of colors, shapes, and sizes. Colors range from basic whites to glowing reds or deep blues. Counter tiles are also glazed, with a semigloss or high-gloss finish that makes it easy to wipe up spills. And, just as for wall tiles, there are a variety of specially shaped trim tiles, some of which are shown below. These special tiles allow the do-it-yourselfer to tile around sinks, along counter edges, and around corners, or to install a tile backsplash.

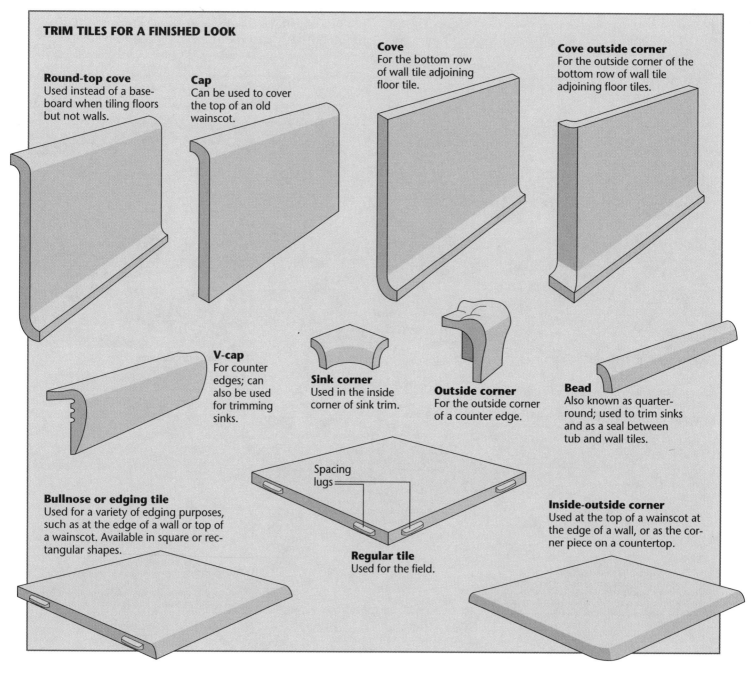

TRIM TILES FOR A FINISHED LOOK

Round-top cove
Used instead of a baseboard when tiling floors but not walls.

Cap
Can be used to cover the top of an old wainscot.

Cove
For the bottom row of wall tile adjoining floor tile.

Cove outside corner
For the outside corner of the bottom row of wall tile adjoining floor tiles.

V-cap
For counter edges; can also be used for trimming sinks.

Sink corner
Used in the inside corner of sink trim.

Outside corner
For the outside corner of a counter edge.

Bead
Also known as quarter-round; used to trim sinks and as a seal between tub and wall tiles.

Spacing lugs

Bullnose or edging tile
Used for a variety of edging purposes, such as at the edge of a wall or top of a wainscot. Available in square or rectangular shapes.

Regular tile
Used for the field.

Inside-outside corner
Used at the top of a wainscot at the edge of a wall, or as the corner piece on a countertop.

BUYING TILE

Installing ceramic tile can be a sizable financial commitment. Choosing a tile that meets both functional and decorative needs requires careful thought. Take time to shop around, calculate cost, and order carefully.

SHOPPING AROUND

Ready sources of information are showrooms, decorators and architects, and tile contractors.

Ceramic tile manufacturers, distributors, and dealers, as well as some licensed contractors, have showrooms displaying a great variety of tiles. Not only can you examine the tile, but you can see how it can be used in a sampling of actual situations—especially bathroom and kitchen settings. The showroom staff can answer your questions and advise you on tile selection, the amount of tiles you'll require, and the costs of your project. You can usually borrow samples to try out at home for color, size, and compatibility. Showrooms and the literature they offer can be important sources for ideas on types, colors, and possible patterns. In case you decide not to do the job yourself, most tile dealers have their own installers.

Decorators and architects specialize in combining aesthetics and function. They can help you analyze your particular needs and find solutions to tricky decorating problems.

Tile contractors may show you tile samples and advise you on some basic choices, but you should have your selection already in mind from your own legwork. It's best to get a written estimate of labor costs and of the tile costs if the contractor is purchasing it. The contractor can also advise you on potential structural problems, such as whether your subfloor will support a heavy tile floor. The experienced hand of a licensed tile contractor is best for some projects. For example, installing swimming pool tile is not usually do-it-yourself work. Applications that require setting tiles in a full mortar bed, such as around a free-form or sunken tub, are best handled by a professional. Tile dealers and distributors can arrange a contractor for you, but, if possible, have one recommended by a satisfied customer.

If browsing through catalogs and shopping in showrooms have left you without a satisfactory tile, consider having tile made to order. Customizing tile is done mostly in the glazing process. Custom tile manufacturers will glaze "raw" (unglazed) tiles to the color and pattern of your choice. You can also paint your own tiles and have them glazed. As a less costly alternative, customize tile with decals. There are also special tile manufacturers who create tile in odd shapes and sizes to fill specific custom design needs.

The costs of tile vary from modest to very expensive. Generally the more tiles of a particular size, surface pattern, and glaze that are manufactured, the less each one will cost. Special surface treatment, such as glazing and texturing, and manufacturing in smaller batches, means higher prices.

Single-color, glazed, flat-surfaced tiles—those commonly used around showers and tubs—are the most economical. The trim pieces for these tiles normally cost more per square foot than the regular tiles. The addition of three-dimensional patterns and multicolored glazes can easily double costs, however. Other factors that affect the cost include the purity and density of the clay used and the temperature at which the tiles are baked. Purer clays fired at higher temperatures generally make costlier but better-wearing tiles.

BEFORE YOU BUY

When you're ready to select and purchase your ceramic tile, follow these helpful tips:

• Have accurate measurements prepared for the area to be covered. A plan on graph paper helps you to visualize the area and provides a clue to the trim pieces you may need. Your tile dealer will help you figure out how many tiles you require.

• Most retailers have displays or catalogs of tiles they don't have in stock; you may have to wait a long time for certain styles, so plan accordingly.

• Always buy more tiles than you need—the rule of thumb is to add 5%. This allows for the ones that are cut to the wrong size or that break while cutting. If a tile breaks or chips after installation, you'll have an extra to replace it. If you wait until damage occurs to buy replacement tiles, you may not be able to find pieces that match.

• Before you bring the tiles home, check the cartons to be sure the shades of color in the tile match. Different cartons of the same tile can vary significantly.

📏 ASK A PRO

HOW CAN I SAVE MONEY ON TILE?

One way is to watch for closeouts. A dealer will often sell closeouts at a discount. These may be tiles that the manufacturer has discontinued, a color or pattern that was overstocked, or a supply of tiles left over from a large installation or a cancelled order.

Another way to save money when buying tile is to purchase "seconds." These tiles are flawed or blemished (usually only slightly), so they cannot be sold with the regular stock at full price. Often, seconds will go undetected if randomly mixed with unblemished tile. However, watch out for seconds that have a pitted surface. When grout is spread, it may settle in these tiny holes and give the tiles a mottled look.

ADHESIVES

The traditional method for laying ceramic tile used to be to set the tile in a thick bed of mortar. Nowadays, you can get excellent results by using adhesives. There are many kinds available and they fall into three major categories: mastics, which are a type of glue; thin-sets, which are cement-base; and epoxy, which are chemically activated resins. The advantages and disadvantages of mastics and thin-sets are described below. Epoxy-base adhesives are used primarily for commercial applications which have to withstand very heavy loads and chemical exposure; their use in residential applications has been replaced by the development of latex- and polymer-modified thin-sets.

ASK A PRO

WHAT IF MY FLOOR ISN'T STABLE?
If your floor bounces, or "dances," you should leave the tiling job to a professional. He or she will probably choose the method illustrated below, referred to as a "floating floor." A layer of asphalt felt is put down, then a layer of wire mesh, and then a thick bed of mortar. The felt allows the tile to move independently from the floor so the tile doesn't crack when the floor heaves.

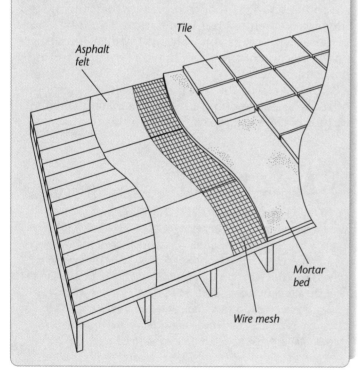

Tile

Asphalt felt

Mortar bed

Wire mesh

As well as ease of application, your choice of adhesive depends on the tile you're using, the backing you're applying it to, and the use you'll make of the finished surface. Check with your dealer to be sure that the adhesive you've selected is appropriate to your application. Adhesives also have different open times (the time you have to set the tiles after the adhesive is applied). A longer open time allows you to set more tiles at once.

Mastics (organic adhesives): Mastics are classified as organic adhesives because they were originally made from rubber-tree extracts. They are the most popular choice with do-it-yourselfers. Essentially a glue, mastics come in a can, premixed in liquid form, and cure by drying. Solvent-base mastics, which give off toxic and flammable fumes, have largely been replaced by mastics with a latex base. The latex helps the mastics spread more easily and makes them somewhat water-resistant.

Mastics are primarily intended for use on walls, but some can be used on floors (check with your dealer). They are most appropriate for use with soft, absorbent tiles. Suitable backings include smooth plaster, gypsum wallboard, or plywood; avoid using them when tiling over concrete or existing tile.

Mastics are cheap and easy to apply. They also offer a longer open time than thin-sets. However, mastics are not absolutely waterproof and are not a good choice for walls that will be frequently subjected to moisture. Another disadvantage of mastics is that they must be applied to a completely dry surface.

Thin-sets (cement-base adhesives): These are known as thin-sets because only a thin layer is used (as opposed to a thick mortar bed); they are also referred to as thin-set mortar. Thin-sets are premixed by the manufacturer and contain portland cement and sand.

Today, most thin-sets come with either a latex or a polymer additive. The latex additive comes in liquid form, while the polymer additive is a dry powder premixed with the thin-set by the manufacturer. Polymer-modified thin-sets have the advantage that you only need to work with one product—just add water—while latex-modified thin-sets involve mixing in the separate liquid latex (you don't add any water).

Thin-sets are more expensive than mastics, but both latex- and polymer-modified thin-sets offer the advantages of being more shock- and water-resistant, and of being usable with a greater variety of backings. They can be applied to a slightly damp surface. Latex-modified thin-sets are more waterproof and more flexible and durable than polymer-modified ones.

Thin-sets can be used with all types of tile. Suitable backings include cured cement slabs if completely free from paint and other coatings, cement backerboard, exterior-grade plywood, gypsum wallboard, ceramic tile, marble, and brick. Some thin-sets don't adhere well to vinyl, asphalt, or linoleum surfaces—check the label.

GROUT, CAULK, AND SEALER

Grout is applied after the tile has been set into place. It highlights the pattern and fills the joints, keeping out foreign matter such as dirt, food, and—if it is sealed—liquids. Caulk is used in joints that require flexibility. In general, unglazed tile and cement-base grouts need to be sealed, whereas glazed tile and epoxy grout do not.

GROUT

Whether you choose a cement-base or an epoxy grout depends on the tile that you're going to use, as well as its location, the width of the joint, and the adhesive. Make sure to check your choice of grout with your tile dealer to be sure that it's appropriate for your particular application.

Grout is available in a wide range of colors. It can be purchased already colored, or you can make up your own color. One caution with dark grout: If you're using unglazed tiles, seal them first. Then test the grout on one of the tiles to make sure that it won't stain. You'll find instructions for applying grout and sealer starting on page 53.

Cement-base grouts: The basic cement grout comes in a bag containing portland cement, which may or may not have sand added to it. You simply add water. This type of grout is cheap but it must be kept damp to cure, and is hard to keep clean. The basic cement grouts are water-resistant, but not absolutely waterproof; you'll need to seal the grout after it has dried for a few days.

As with adhesives, cement-base grout is available with either a latex or a polymer additive; both types cure by drying. These modified grouts are more water-resistant than the basic cement grout; they also dry more slowly and are easier to clean up. Polymer- and latex-modified grouts are water-resistant and can be sealed to increase stain-resistance. The polymer additive is a dry powder that is mixed with the cement by the manufacturer; all you have to do is add water to the dry mix. The main disadvantage of polymer-modified grout is that it is not very resistant to the chemicals in spills such as food or urine. Latex-modified grouts incorporate a liquid latex additive. They offer a longer open time than polymer-modified grouts, are more resistant to chemicals and more colorfast, and result in a stronger bond.

Epoxy grouts: Although epoxy grouts are highly waterproof, their main advantage over thin-sets is that they are highly resistant to most chemicals and stains. This makes epoxy a good choice in a kitchen, workroom, or darkroom, or on a countertop. Epoxy grouts are also very colorfast. You can use epoxy grouts with any tile adhesive, but they are more expensive than other types of grout. They can be toxic during application and safety precautions must be followed when working with them (*right*). Epoxy grouts do not need to be sealed.

SILICONE RUBBER CAULK

Commonly known as bathtub caulk, silicone rubber caulk stays permanently flexible, withstands extremes of cold and heat, repels water, and resists mildew. It comes in tubes or cartridges and is squeezed into the joints, instead of being spread over the tile as is grout.

Silicone rubber caulk is used for flexible joints where surfaces tend to move slightly or where there may be water seepage, such as where a wall meets a floor, where tiles abut wood trim, and around bathtubs and sinks.

SEALER

Unglazed tile (except for porcelain tile) should be sealed. Cement-base grout should be sealed where it might be stained, such as on a kitchen floor. You can also use a sealer to increase the water-resistance of cement-base grout in shower and tub surrounds. If you're sealing both the tile and the grout, select a sealer compatible with both. You can choose between topical or penetrating sealers. Topical sealers can be used with all unglazed tile to protect the tile and provide a surface finish. Although porcelain tile does not need to be sealed, you can apply a topical sealer for a smoother finish. Topical sealers need to be stripped and reapplied periodically. Penetrating sealers soak into the tile and protect it permanently; they can be used for all unglazed tile and are the best choice for soft tile, such as Mexican tile, and for all outdoor tile. If you're installing glazed tile, seal the grout only. Silicone grout sealers will wear off with time and should not be used where there might be contact with food. Solvent- and water-base penetrating sealers are also available.

PLAY IT SAFE

WORKING WITH EPOXY GROUT

When using epoxy grout, always follow the safety directions given on the package. Avoid breathing the fumes or contacting the grout with your skin. The grout can damage your eyes if it splashes; always wear eye protection. Work in a well-ventilated area and wear rubber gloves and long sleeves. If you find you're sensitive to the epoxy, wear a respirator (check with your local safety equipment supplier for the appropriate cartridge and filter). Alternatively, you could switch to a different type of adhesive, or hire a contractor to complete the job.

TOOLS AND TECHNIQUES

Most of the tools required for installing ceramic tile are general-purpose tools you may already have; these are shown below. You'll also need a few tools specifically for ceramic tile work *(opposite)*. If you have to cut very heavy tile, consider renting a wet saw from your dealer. In addition to the tools shown, you will need some basic carpentry tools for installing new backings (which could be plywood, wallboard, or cement backerboard), for trimming doors and casings, and for fastening wood battens to the existing floor.

Starting on page 27, we'll show you some of the techniques you'll need for your project. You'll need some carpentry skills; these are not covered in this book.

Before you undertake your tiling project, be prepared with the appropriate safety equipment:
• Safety goggles or safety glasses: Wear when using any striking tool, and when working with a material that could splash, such as adhesive or grout.
• Work gloves: Wear when working with sharp or rough materials.
• Rubber gloves: Wear when working with caustic products such as epoxy grout.
• Dust mask: Wear when working with dusty materials, such as dry adhesive or grout.
• Respirator: Wear when using products that give off toxic fumes, such as epoxy grout.

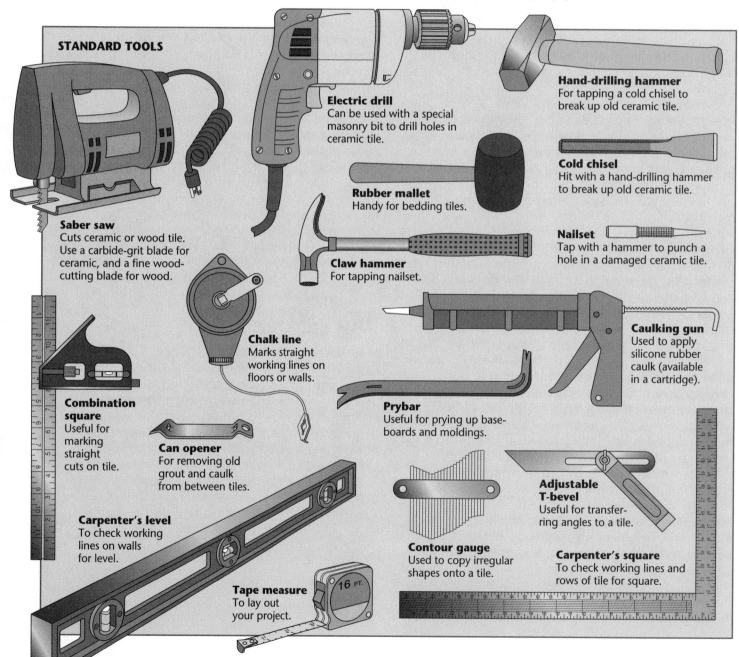

STANDARD TOOLS

Electric drill
Can be used with a special masonry bit to drill holes in ceramic tile.

Hand-drilling hammer
For tapping a cold chisel to break up old ceramic tile.

Cold chisel
Hit with a hand-drilling hammer to break up old ceramic tile.

Rubber mallet
Handy for bedding tiles.

Saber saw
Cuts ceramic or wood tile. Use a carbide-grit blade for ceramic, and a fine wood-cutting blade for wood.

Claw hammer
For tapping nailset.

Nailset
Tap with a hammer to punch a hole in a damaged ceramic tile.

Chalk line
Marks straight working lines on floors or walls.

Caulking gun
Used to apply silicone rubber caulk (available in a cartridge).

Combination square
Useful for marking straight cuts on tile.

Can opener
For removing old grout and caulk from between tiles.

Prybar
Useful for prying up base-boards and moldings.

Adjustable T-bevel
Useful for transferring angles to a tile.

Carpenter's level
To check working lines on walls for level.

Contour gauge
Used to copy irregular shapes onto a tile.

Carpenter's square
To check working lines and rows of tile for square.

Tape measure
To lay out your project.

TOOLS OF THE TRADE: CERAMIC TILE

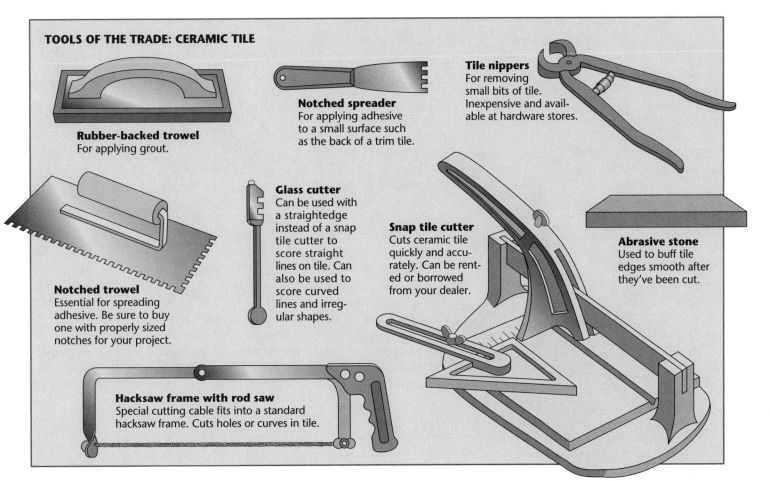

Rubber-backed trowel
For applying grout.

Notched spreader
For applying adhesive to a small surface such as the back of a trim tile.

Tile nippers
For removing small bits of tile. Inexpensive and available at hardware stores.

Glass cutter
Can be used with a straightedge instead of a snap tile cutter to score straight lines on tile. Can also be used to score curved lines and irregular shapes.

Snap tile cutter
Cuts ceramic tile quickly and accurately. Can be rented or borrowed from your dealer.

Abrasive stone
Used to buff tile edges smooth after they've been cut.

Notched trowel
Essential for spreading adhesive. Be sure to buy one with properly sized notches for your project.

Hacksaw frame with rod saw
Special cutting cable fits into a standard hacksaw frame. Cuts holes or curves in tile.

Marking tile

TOOLKIT
- Contour gauge for irregular shapes
- Adjustable T-bevel for angles

Marking border tiles
If your tiles have ridged backs, mark cuts parallel to the ridges. To mark for straight cuts, place the tile, finished surface up, exactly on top of the last full tile that you have set. Then place another tile on top of this one, with one edge butted against the wall. Using the edge of the top tile as a guide, mark the cut-off line with a fine felt-tip pen. This method is illustrated on page 78. To mark a tile for a corner, use this process twice—once on each wall. See page 79 for an illustration.

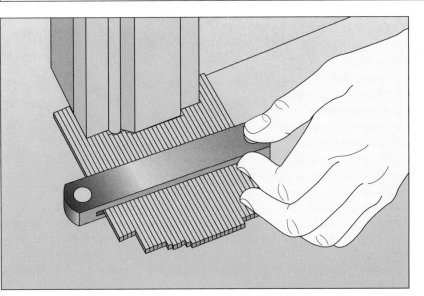

Marking irregular shapes
To fit a tile to an irregular contour, match it with a contour gauge (left) and transfer the outline to the tile with a felt-tip pen. You can also cut a pattern from cardboard and then transfer the shape to the tile.

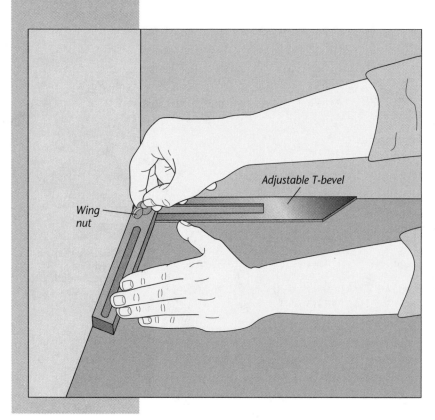

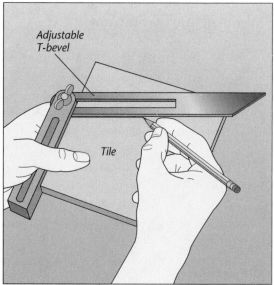

Transferring an angle
To set the adjustable T-bevel, loosen the wing nut, set the tool to fit the angle of the surface and tighten the wing nut *(left)*; copy the angle onto the tile *(above)*. For a 90° cut, use a combination square.

Cutting ceramic tile

TOOLKIT

For straight cuts:
• Snap tile cutter
OR
• Glass cutter and straightedge
OR
• Wet saw
For interior cuts:
• Electric drill with masonry bit
• Hacksaw frame with rod saw
For irregular shapes:
• Tile nippers

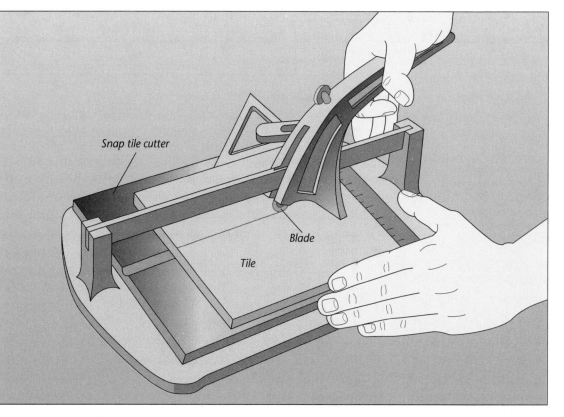

Cutting straight lines
To use a snap tile cutter, first position the tile. Score the surface by pulling the handle toward you while pressing down firmly. Then, press down on the handle to break the tile. Another way to cut tile in a straight line is to use a glass cutter and straightedge. Score the tile, then place the scored line over a dowel and press down evenly on both edges.

To remove a thin strip of tile near the edge, use tile nippers *(opposite)*. If you want to cut a narrow piece, use a wet saw.

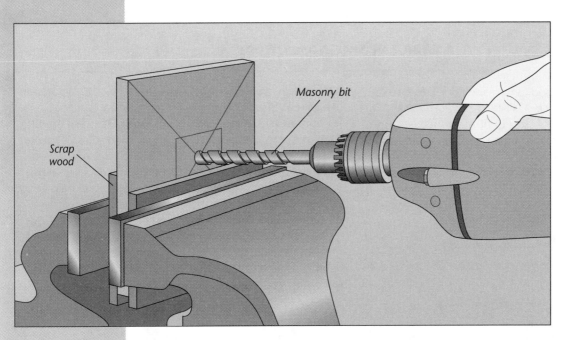

Scrap wood

Masonry bit

Making interior cuts

To make a cut within a tile, first drill through it using an electric drill with a masonry bit *(left)*. If the tile is held in a vise, protect it with a piece of scrap wood on each side. If you don't have a vise, clamp the tile to the edge of a table, protecting the tile with pieces of wood.

After the hole is drilled, pass the rod saw through the hole and hook it to your hacksaw frame, then cut the desired shape *(below)*.

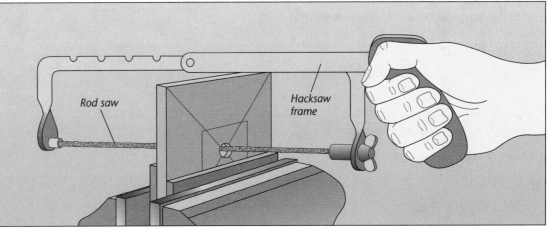

Rod saw

Hacksaw frame

Tile nippers

Cutting away small bits of tile

Use tile nippers to cut both irregular shapes and straight lines near the edge of the tile. If a narrow edge of tile must be cut in a straight line, first score the tile with the snap tile cutter; for irregular or curved lines, score the line with a glass cutter. Then nibble your way up to the line with tile nippers *(left)*. Don't try to cut on the line the first time; cut slightly short and then carefully work up to it. Too big a bite the first time usually results in chipping beyond the line. If you're removing a thin strip of tile, start from the corners to avoid chipping.

Smoothing

After a tile is snapped or nipped, remove any rough or jagged edges with a special abrasive stone, or with a small piece of concrete. You can also smooth the edges by rubbing the tile against a whetstone.

By far the simplest method for spacing floor tiles is to use the molded plastic spacers available from your dealer. They come in a wide variety of sizes to fit many needs. Large plastic spacers can be placed on end as shown below *(bottom)*; they can be removed easily before grouting. Smaller plastic spacers can be placed at each corner but these are more difficult to remove and, if left in, will still show once the grout is applied. You can also use scraps of plywood, which work well with joints of ¼ inch or wider.

Or you can use a tile stick, as shown below *(right)* to space the tiles. A tile stick is usable for joints of any size.

Some wall tiles are made with lugs that space the tiles. Others come with plastic spacers like floor tiles. If spacers are not available, you can use finishing nails of the right diameter *(page 40)*. Wall tiles can also be spaced and aligned by using cord or rope pulled tight between two nails at the ends of each course, as shown below *(left)*. Use nylon cord to prevent any fibers from sticking in the adhesive.

Mosaics come already spaced and mounted on a mesh backing. Lay down one or two square feet of these tiles at a time, adding spacing only between each new section.

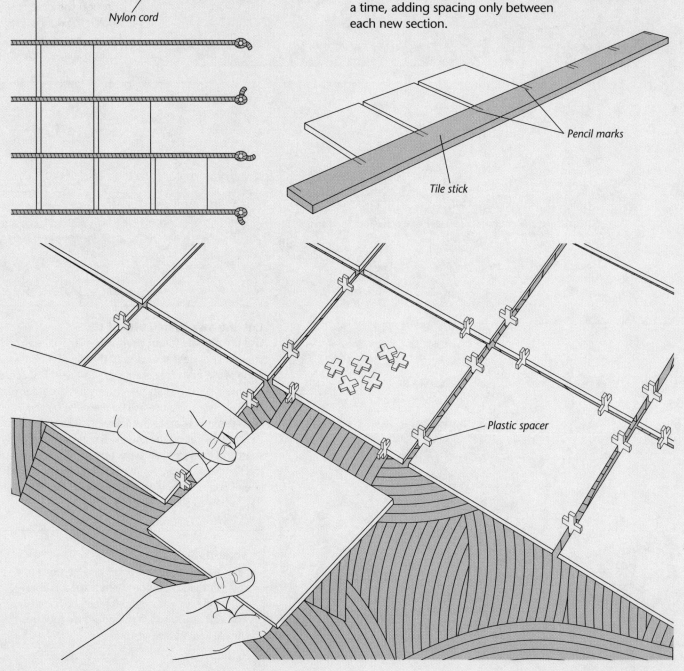

Nylon cord

Pencil marks

Tile stick

Plastic spacer

PREPARING THE SURFACE

Of all the steps in successful tile installation, probably the most important is preparing the backing—the material over which the tile will be placed. The composition and structural soundness of this surface not only determines the quality and durability of the finished tile surface, but a thorough job of installing or preparing the backing will save you time and money later. Existing backings must be solid, flat, smooth, and clean; if you're using mastic, they must also be dry. Don't try to install tile over a springy surface. If the surface gives under pressure, replace it or cover it with a smooth, rigid surface. Any movement will cause the grout and tile to crack. If there is a great deal of bounce in the floor, you may need to have a professional install a "floating floor" (page 24).

You can install ceramic tile directly over many existing floor and wall backings, such as old ceramic tile, resilient flooring, smooth plaster, brick, plywood, and concrete. If you need to install new backing, plywood, gypsum wallboard, cement backerboard, a mortar bed, or a concrete slab are all good choices. Each type is discussed below. NOTE: Not all types of adhesive can be used with all types of backings; check with your dealer whether your adhesive and backing are compatible.

The backing should be flat within 1/8 inch over 10 feet. If your backing doesn't come within these limits, you may be able either to sand out the bumps or to fill the dips with thin-set adhesive, which dries hard and smooth; do not use mastics for filling dips. To check a floor for dips, run a long straightedge over the floor and look at it against the light for gaps under the straightedge. Mark the outer edges of the dip with pencil and then fill by troweling in a thin-set adhesive. After the adhesive has dried, use an abrasive stone to smooth out the filler along the edges. If the existing surface is badly cracked or broken, loose, very irregular, or otherwise in poor condition, replace it or cover with a new backing.

In areas that have to withstand a lot of moisture, such as in a shower or tub enclosure, the best choice of backing is cement backerboard (page 32), which will not disintegrate when wet. To keep all moisture out of the wall, put a moisture barrier over the wall studs; in addition, you can apply a waterproof membrane over the backing. Make sure that the membrane you plan to use is appropriate for your application. Waterproof membrane comes in a kit consisting of reinforcing fabric and liquid rubber; follow the manufacturer's instructions to apply it. You can tile directly over the membrane. If you choose to use gypsum wallboard in a damp area, make sure it is the water-resistant type.

Concrete: An existing concrete subfloor must be flat, smooth, clean, and free of cracks. A slightly damp surface does not pose a problem with a thin-set adhesive. Remove grease and oil stains with a chemical garage-floor cleaner, available at most auto supply stores. Chip or scrape off any excess concrete, paint, or other foreign material. If the concrete surface is glossy, waxed, sealed, painted, or shows signs of efflorescence, the adhesive won't bond well. To test, sprinkle some water on the concrete; if it beads, the floor should be sanded with a rented floor sander fitted with No. 4 or 5 open-cut sandpaper. Finish by vacuuming up all loose material and then damp-mopping up the dust.

Fill all the holes and low areas with a good concrete patching material available at most home centers, or with the thin-set adhesive that you'll use for the tile. Expansion joints should be caulked, not filled, and should not be tiled over. The floor must be flat.

If your concrete floor is rough, uneven, or in poor condition, consider having a new concrete surface placed

QUICK FIX

BRIDGING CRACKS IN CONCRETE
Hairline cracks can be bridged by applying a commercial crack-suppression membrane (right). These kits contain a fabric tape and liquid rubber. The tile bonds to the membrane instead of to the concrete. The width of the membrane should exceed the width of the tile being used. Large cracks in concrete may indicate a structural problem, such as movement (if one side of the crack is higher than the other).

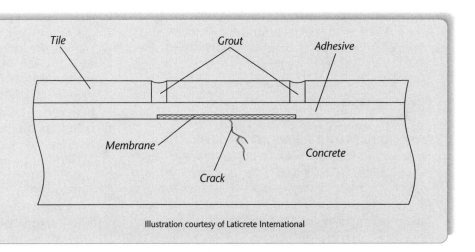

Illustration courtesy of Laticrete International

over it. In placing a new slab for a tile base, be sure to install a plastic moisture barrier over the old slab and reinforce the slab thoroughly to prevent any cracking (consult a professional for directions). Finish the slab with a light brooming to give it a slightly rough texture, which will make the adhesive bond well to it.

Wood and plywood: Whether it is a floor, wall, or countertop, a wood surface must be very smooth, and this generally means that you'll use plywood. Plywood underlayment applied over a subfloor is a suitable backing; exterior-grade plywood or Exposure 1 plywood, which have water-resistant glues, should always be used. Most other wood surfaces, such as planks or tongue-and-groove boards, are not smooth or strong enough and should be covered with plywood. NOTE: Do not use particleboard, oriented-strand board (OSB), or lauan as backing for tile.

For tile floors, the thickness of the subfloor and underlayment combined should be 1¹/₄ inches. This will prevent flexing, which can crack tile and grout. Ideally, each layer should be ⁵/₈ inch—the thickness of the tongue-and-groove plywood commonly used for subfloors in recent construction. However, if the subfloor is thick enough, the underlayment can be a minimum of ³/₈ inch. If you're not sure how thick your subfloor is (older houses often have ³/₄-inch boards), drill a hole in the floor and measure. A floor that isn't thick enough is subject to flexing. Adjacent edges of plywood subfloors must not be above or below each other by more than ¹/₃₂ inch. If your subfloor and underlayment are not thick enough, put down an additional layer of ³/₈-inch exterior-grade plywood. If there is any doubt as to the suitability of your existing floor, consult a professional.

When putting down plywood over existing plywood subfloors, the middle of the new sheet should cover the butted ends of the existing plywood. Stagger the new panels so that the four corners do not line up *(page 74)*. Leave a slight gap—about ¹/₈ inch—between adjacent panels to permit expansion. Nail panels to the subfloor with ring-shank nails twice as long as the new plywood is thick. Space the nails 6 inches apart along the edges and 8 inches apart in the field, following the floor joists if possible.

For countertops, use a minimum of ³/₄-inch exterior plywood. Make sure it is firmly supported by the cabi-

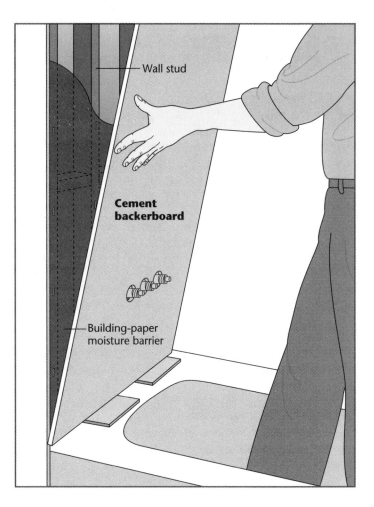

Wall stud

Cement backerboard

Building-paper moisture barrier

nets and is screwed into the top edges of the cabinet every 6 inches.

Cement backerboard: The technical name for cement backerboard, also known as backerboard, is concrete glassfiber-reinforced backerboard. Essentially a thin piece of concrete sandwiched between pieces of fiberglass mesh, this material combines the water-resistant qualities of mortar and the easy installation of gypsum wallboard. Cement backerboard can be used to cover existing gypsum wallboard; it won't disintegrate or swell if it gets wet. To keep moisture out, cover the cement backerboard with a waterproof membrane, as described on page 31.

Cement backerboard usually comes in the form of panels ⁷/₁₆ inch thick and ranges in size from 3 by 4 feet to 3 by 6 feet. It is fastened to wall studs or over existing wallboard with 1¹/₂-inch galvanized screws. With a cement-base adhesive, seal joints between panels and between panel and tub or shower receptor, as well as any other openings. Tape corners with 2-inch-wide coated fiberglass tape embedded in a thin coat of mortar.

Cement backerboard can be installed over plywood subfloors for additional strength and water-resistance. The boards will not support any load by themselves on a horizontal surface. For maximum resistance to flexing, glue the cement backerboard to the subfloor with a cement-base adhesive and then fasten every

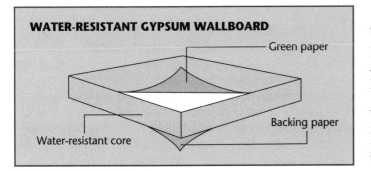

Green paper

Backing paper

Water-resistant core

6 inches with 1¹/₂-inch galvanized screws. Fill gaps between the panels with the same adhesive used to set the tiles. Use thin-set as the tile adhesive.

Gypsum wallboard: Also called drywall, gypsum wallboard is the most common existing wall surface. Because the gypsum core disintegrates if it gets damp, standard gypsum wallboard (which has a gray paper covering) shouldn't be used in wet areas unless covered with a waterproof membrane *(page 31)*. Most new bathrooms are covered with a water-resistant gypsum wallboard, which has a green or blue paper covering *(above)*. To minimize water penetration, use a polymer- or latex-modified thin-set to seal the grout. The wall should be clean and free of wallpaper, which heavy tile will pull loose. Clean dirt and grease from gypsum board walls with a cleaner such as TSP (trisodium phosphate). Remove loose or flaking paint with a wire brush; roughen the finish if it's glossy. Sanding will do both jobs. Fill any cracks, gouges, or holes with a patching compound. Remove any wallpaper. If the wallboard is damaged, mildewed, or crumbly, it must be torn out and replaced with a new backing.

Use screws, nails, or adhesive to fasten gypsum wallboard to existing walls or studs. Using tape and special joint compound, according to the instructions of the gypsum board manufacturer, tape all joints between panels; cover all nailheads, and seal all cut edges.

Resilient flooring: A variety of materials, including vinyl and cork, are used as resilient flooring. Some make good backings if smooth, clean, and tightly in place. Be sure that the subfloor and underlayment combined are 1¹/₄ inch thick; drill a small hole to check. Cushioned vinyl, a common sheet vinyl covering, is not a good backing because it allows some flexing, which cracks grout and tile. Cushioned vinyl floors can be covered with ³/₈-inch exterior plywood. Cork flooring is also a poor backing as it compresses too easily. If you're considering removing an old resilient floor, read the safety information *(below, left)*.

Ceramic tile: Existing ceramic tile may be used as backing for new ceramic tiles. But make sure the old tile is in good condition, well bonded, and clean.

Loose tiles often mean water has penetrated the grout or has leaked from behind and weakened the backing. Remove any loose tiles and examine the backing; pull off any suspect tiles. It's easier to replace a questionable tile now than to do the job over later. If there's no problem, clean the old adhesive from the tile and backing, and replace with new adhesive. If you find damp gypsum wallboard behind wall tiles, remove all the tiles and replace the old backing. If there are many loose or broken tiles, it's best to remove them all. If the old tile is on a plywood-backed countertop, use a cold chisel and hammer—wear safety goggles—to break it out; then scrape and sand the surface until smooth. It may be easier to apply a new top. For walls, pull out the wallboard and tile and install either waterproof gypsum wallboard or cement backerboard for the new backing. Be sure to protect the shower or tub area against scratches or chips.

To place new tile over old, first clean the old tile thoroughly to remove soap scum, mineral buildup, coatings, wax, and dirt. Use a degreasing product such as TSP. Test the surface by applying the adhesive to a 1-foot-square area. If it hasn't bonded well by the next day, use an abrasive disc mounted on an electric drill to roughen the old tile. Wear a good dust mask as you work and remove all dust afterward.

One more factor to consider is whether to stop at the height of the existing tile or to continue up to the ceiling. If you're stopping with the old tile, cover the edge with a cap tile *(page 22)*. To tile to the ceiling, install new backing above the old. Shim the backing if necessary to make it flush with the old tile.

Mortar bed: The traditional backing for tile is a mortar bed. Its value is that curves and coves can be built into counters, shower pans, or around sinks to give the tile a unique look. Consider having a professional lay the mortar bed and then tile it yourself.

If you intend to tile both walls and floors, begin with the walls (page 38). This is necessary if you're using cove tile at the bottom of the wall; if not, this sequence is still more convenient. If you're only tiling the floor, you can use a round-top cove (page 22) instead of a baseboard.

To prepare the working area, clear away rugs, furniture, and any other obstacles. Cover adjacent finished areas with paper or plastic sheeting. Remove baseboards; if this is difficult (especially in older homes with plaster walls) and there is quarter-round shoe molding next to the baseboard, just remove that and tile up to the baseboard. Use a thin-blade prybar or a butt chisel. Leave room for a grout joint between the tile and baseboard. Any irregularities can be covered when the shoe molding is replaced. For bathrooms, remove the vanity or pedestal washbasin and the floor-mounted toilet bowl.

Before you begin, make sure that the backing is rigid, flat, smooth, and clean; see page 31. (If you're using a mastic, the surface must also be dry.) Check that tile colors match from box to box; slight variations are one of the charms of tile, but you may prefer uniformity. Make sure that the adhesive is compatible with your backing and that the grout will work with the adhesive and tiles. Many tiles, particularly those with reddish bodies, can be dusty. This dust can prevent adhesives from bonding to the tiles. If necessary, brush them clean.

Once your surface and materials are ready, the first step is to mark working lines. Working lines are laid out on the subfloor to keep your first tile course straight and to adjust for any crookedness in the room walls. Laying out accurate working lines seems tedious, but doing this job right will make the rest go faster and smoother.

Two basic methods are used to establish working lines. In one, a chalk line is snapped down the center of the room; in the other, chalk lines are snapped near a wall. If your room is badly out of square or if you want a decorative design or pattern symmetrically located, start in the center. This usually means having cut tiles along all four walls. The layout of working lines (square or diagonal) and the tiling sequence for resilient tile are described on page 75; follow the same steps for ceramic.

Many professional tile installers use the method explained on the opposite page. This involves starting from one wall and usually means that tiles will have to be cut along two walls. If possible, plan to put the rows of cut tiles where they'll be least noticeable. This method can only be used if two walls meet at 90°.

If you've picked tiles that are not square or rectangular, such as ogee or Moorish, you may have to adjust the working lines. Make a dry run (without adhesive). Before tiling, decide on the tile bond, or pattern; the joints can be lined up or the rows staggered (page 40).

ASK A PRO

HOW DO I PLAN FOR DOORWAYS?

Where tile ends in a doorway or similar opening, there is often a difference in height between the tile surface and the adjoining floor. If the tile is higher, you can finish off the edge with bullnose tiles. These have a curved edge that creates a smooth transition between the two levels. When a tile floor meets a carpeted area, the levels may be roughly the same, so regular square-edge tiles may do the job. With mosaic tile, a marble threshold (available from your dealer) is often used to make a transition between two levels.

New tile on the floor may mean you'll have to trim the doors to allow for the added height. To determine where the door must be cut, place a tile plus a 1/8-inch spacer, such as a piece of cardboard, on the floor against the door. Mark the door as shown at right. On exterior doors, allow for weather stripping on the bottom edge of the door. Remove any doors that open into the room by tapping out the hinge pins (don't unscrew the hinges) and cut with a fine-toothed saw. To minimize splintering, cover the cut line on both sides with masking tape.

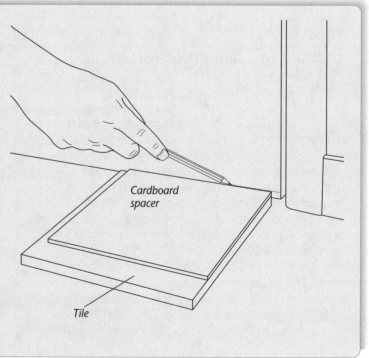

Cardboard spacer

Tile

Laying out floor tiles

TOOLKIT
• Chalk line
• Tape measure
• Carpenter's square
• Tile stick (optional)

1 ▶ Checking for square
The easiest place to start tiling is from a straight wall adjoining a square corner. Check the room for square corners and straight walls by placing a tile firmly against the wall in each corner of the room. Snap a chalk line along the outside edges of the tiles from one corner to the next *(right)*. Variations in the distance between chalk line and wall will show any crookedness in the wall. Variations about the width of a grout joint can be tolerated, since baseboards and shoe moldings can cover some irregularities; anything bigger must be cut. Using a carpenter's square, see if the lines at any corner intersect at right angles.

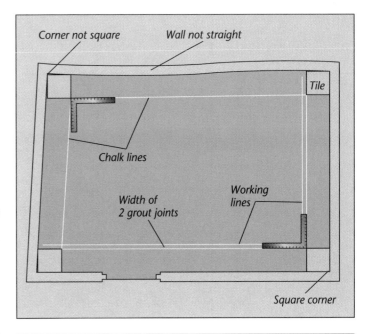

Corner not square   *Wall not straight*

Tile

Chalk lines

Width of 2 grout joints

Working lines

Square corner

2 Laying a dry run
Before you mark working lines, make a dry run (lay the tile out on the floor) to help determine the best layout and minimize the number of cut tiles. Use spacers or a tile stick *(page 30)* to help you achieve uniform spacing. Sometimes, a slight alteration of joint widths can eliminate a row of cut tiles. (Grout joints can be increased or decreased slightly along their entire length, but must be straight.)

3 Marking working lines
First select the walls to use as guides (straight walls meeting at 90° are best) and pick one to begin on. If all four walls are square, start where you want to have full tiles; cut tiles along the other walls can be hidden by furniture. On the side of the line away from the wall you're starting with, snap another chalk line parallel to the first one, spaced the width of two grout joints. This allows for a grout joint along the wall to hide variations in straightness and permit expansion, and also for the grout joint between the first two rows of tiles. Repeat this with the chalk line along the other wall; these are your working lines. Fasten a wood batten (1x2 or 1x3) along each line to get rigid guides to butt the tiles against. Make sure the battens in a corner form a right angle. If they don't, check your measurements and adjust as needed. For a concrete floor, you may want to rely on chalk lines only.

Setting floor tiles

TOOLKIT
• Notched trowel
• Tile stick (optional)
• Carpenter's square
• Hammer or rubber mallet

1 Applying adhesive
The manufacturer's instructions will tell you how to mix the adhesive and what size notched trowel you need to produce the correct thickness of the adhesive layer. Check the notch size by setting a tile in adhesive, then removing it. If there are gaps in the adhesive on the back of the tile, the notches are too small. If adhesive squeezes out the edges of the tile, the notches are too big. The label will give the open time—from 5 to 45 minutes.

All adhesives, whether thin-set or mastic, are applied in basically the same way. Pour a small amount of adhesive on the backing or use a putty knife to scoop adhesive out of a bucket. Using the flat edge of the trowel to form a very thin layer, spread the adhesive over the backing. Apply a second layer with the notched side of the trowel; keep the trowel at a 45° to 60° angle and press it firmly against the backing to form ridges in the adhesive. Work back and forth in a crosshatch pattern. With button-back tiles, use a deeper layer of adhesive.

Don't spread more adhesive than you can tile in about 15 minutes, or can comfortably reach over. If a skin appears on the surface, scrape up the adhesive and apply new adhesive.

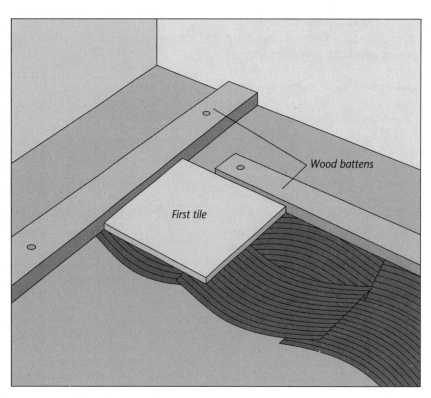

First tile

Wood battens

2 Placing the first tile

Place the first tile with a gentle rocking motion into the corner formed by the two battens. Never slide tile on the adhesive; this pushes the adhesive up between the joints. Make sure the tile is butted tightly against the wood guides, as shown at left. For large tiles—10" by 10" or larger—spread a little adhesive on the back of the tile before setting it.

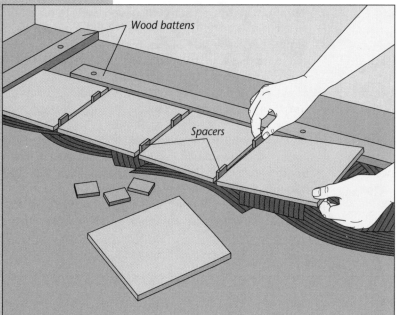

Wood battens

Spacers

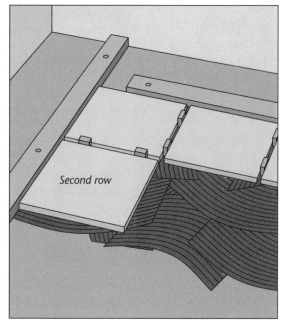

Second row

3 Continuing the rows

With the same motion, place the second tile alongside the first, against the spacers, and continue along the row. Floor tiles seldom have spacing lugs, so use a few pieces of properly sized wood (above, left), molded plastic spacers, or a tile stick to establish the width of the grout joint. The best way to use molded spacers is to push one end into the joint and leave the rest sticking up for easy removal later on. It's not necessary to fit them into the corners between each tile. As you go along, clean off any adhesive that may be spilled on the surface of the tiles.

Continue setting tiles and spacers until you reach the other end of the room. If necessary, mark and cut the last tile (page 27). If you're using a running bond pattern (page 40), start the second row—and every other one—with the first tile spaced one-half the width of a tile from the batten guide. Whichever pattern you choose, begin each new row from the same side of the room as the first one (above, right). Once you've finished a section, remove the spacers.

Try to stay off the tile surface as you work. When you get to the last few rows, lay down pieces of plywood over the tiles to distribute your weight.

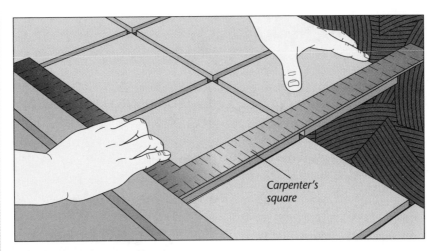

4 Checking for square
From time to time, check with a carpenter's square to make sure that the courses are straight *(left)*. If some of the tiles are out of line, just wiggle them back into position.

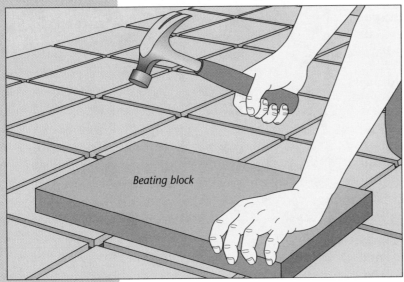

Beating block

5 Bedding the tiles
After you've laid a section, the tiles should be bedded, a process that sets the tile firmly in the adhesive and levels each one with its neighbors. Do this with a rubber mallet or by hammering lightly on a block of wood large enough to cover more than one tile at once *(left)*. As you move the block about, be careful not to push any of the tiles out of line.

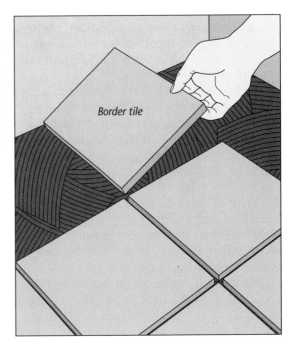

Border tile

6 Laying border tiles
After you set the last row, begin laying the border tiles in the same corner that you started in *(right)*. Carefully remove the battens and spread adhesive in the areas not yet tiled. Work toward the ends, using spacers and bedding the tiles as you move along. You should have a grout line between the border tiles and between the border and the wall. You'll probably have to cut tiles along two walls *(page 27)*. When you've finished, clean off the surface of the tiles.

7 Finishing the project
Stay off the tiles at least overnight—longer if recommended by the adhesive manufacturer. To keep tiles from breaking, keep all but essential traffic off the floor until you grout the joints.

After the adhesive has fully set, apply the grout *(page 53)*. If there is no baseboard or shoe molding to be set on top of the tiles along the wall, fill the space around the perimeter with a flexible silicone rubber caulk.

When the grout is fully cured, wash the surface with detergent or household cleaner and a small amount of water. If your floor is going to be subject to stains, seal the grout, as described on page 53.

If necessary, trim door bottoms so each door clears the tiles; reinstall the doors. After the grout has dried, replace the baseboards and any shoe molding that you removed.

If you're planning to tile both the walls and the floors of a room, always begin with the walls. In a bathroom, begin with the tub enclosure *(page 42)*. To plan your layout, you can mark out an equivalent area on the floor.

To prepare a wall for tiling, remove anything attached to the wall, such as towel bars and paper holders. Then remove faceplates for electrical switches and outlets. Unscrew any electrical device from its box, as shown at right. Cut your tile to fit around the box. CAUTION: When you're removing any electrical device, first turn off the circuit; after you've removed the device, tape the terminals with electrician's tape before turning the circuit back on. To reduce the risk of fire, the box must not be more than ¼ inch back from the finished wall. Once you've finished tiling, install a box extension *(right, inset)* with washers between the old box and the box extension to hold the extension at the right depth. Screw the device through the extension into the original box so that the tabs sit against the face of the tile. Then replace the faceplate.

To tile the walls of a bathroom, remove any wall-mounted basin or toilet—you may want to consult a professional plumber for help in removing and reinstalling plumbing fixtures.

The baseboards can be left in place, with tile starting above them, or you can choose to remove the baseboards and shoe molding, if any. Most baseboards and shoe moldings are attached with finishing nails and can be removed in two ways. One way is to hammer a thin, broad-bladed prybar or chisel gently behind the molding and pry carefully outward until that section of molding is loose. Repeat the process a few feet farther along until that piece can be removed. The other method, which reduces the chances of splitting the molding, is to find the nails and drive them through the molding with a narrow nailset.

The wall surface to be tiled must be firm, clean, and flat, and if you're using a mastic, it must be very dry. It can be of any of the materials discussed starting on page 31. Remove any wallpaper; it may loosen and peel off, taking your new tiles with it. Painted surfaces are acceptable as long as the paint is not flaking. Be sure to clean off dirt and grease and roughen shiny areas. Wash the walls with a good household cleaner, such as TSP (trisodium phosphate, available in hardware stores) to remove grease film, which can impair the adhesive.

If your project includes adding any new electrical outlets or installing a recessed cabinet in the wall, now is the time to do the work inside the wall. If you need help with these jobs, consult a professional electrician or carpenter.

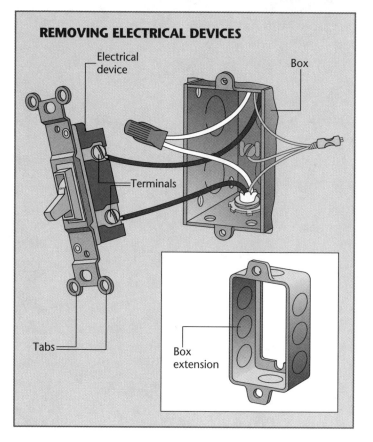

REMOVING ELECTRICAL DEVICES

Electrical device

Box

Terminals

Tabs

Box extension

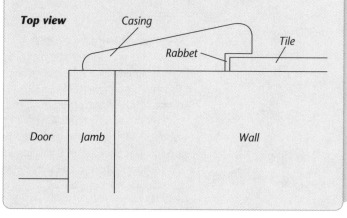

ASK A PRO

DO I NEED TO REMOVE DOOR AND WINDOW CASINGS TO TILE A WALL?
You don't need to remove a window or door casing; just tile up to it, leaving enough space for a flexible joint. However, in some situations, running the tile behind the casing will eliminate an awkward tile cut. If this is necessary, carefully remove the casing and then cut a rabbet in the back, as shown below, to allow room for the tile. You can do this neatly with a router or table saw.

Top view

Casing

Rabbet

Tile

Door

Jamb

Wall

Laying out wall tiles

TOOLKIT
- Carpenter's level
- Straightedge
- Tape measure
- Tile stick

1 Marking the horizontal working line

This line makes the first course of tile level, even if the floor isn't. The line is usually established near the floor. (For tiling around a tub enclosure, see page 42.)

Find the floor's lowest point by setting the level on the floor at various locations against the walls to be tiled. At the lowest point, place a tile against the wall, as shown below. (If the installation will have a cove base, set a cove tile on the floor and a wall tile above it.) Measure up two grout joints above the top of the tile (or use two spacers). Using the carpenter's level and a long straightedge, draw a horizontal line from this point across the wall. Continue it along all walls to be tiled, but double-check your work; it's easy to get a little off level.

After marking your horizontal working lines, nail battens (lengths of 1x3 will do) to the walls. Their top edges should be on the line.

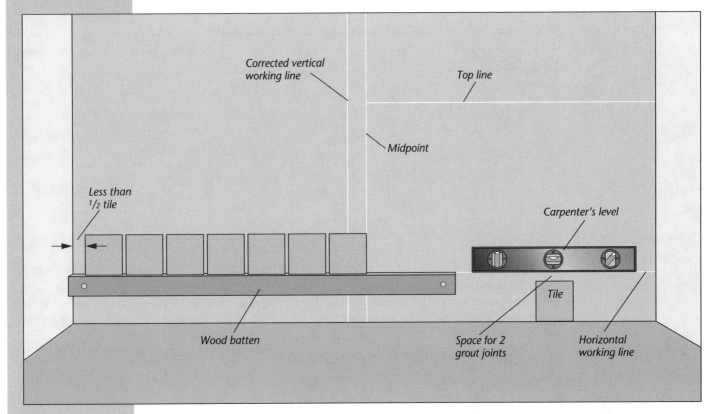

Corrected vertical working line

Top line

Midpoint

Less than ½ tile

Carpenter's level

Tile

Wood batten

Space for 2 grout joints

Horizontal working line

2 Marking the vertical working line

Measure to find the midpoint of a wall and mark it on the horizontal line. Starting at this midpoint, measure with the tile stick or set a row of loose tiles on the batten *(above)* to determine the size of the end tiles. Be sure to allow for the grout joints. If the end tiles will be less than half a tile, move your midpoint mark one-half a tile in either direction to avoid narrow end pieces. Then use the level and straightedge to mark a vertical line through the mark. Repeat the process with the other walls.

3 Marking the top line

If you don't plan to tile all the way to the ceiling, mark where you want to stop. Usually, a tile wainscot extends to a height of about 4'. With your tile stick *(page 30)*, mark the top of the uppermost tile on your vertical line, including the bullnose tile. Use a carpenter's level to check for level and mark a horizontal top line through this point across the wall *(above)*. Repeat the process for the other walls.

4 Marking for accessories

For bathroom walls, lay out the locations of towel bars, paper holders, and soap and toothbrush holders. Mark them on the backing. (Later on, you'll cut tile to fit around the marks, allowing for grout joints). These accessories are heavy and must be installed after the rest of the tile so they can be taped in place while the adhesive dries.

Setting wall tiles

TOOLKIT
• Notched trowel
• Carpenter's square
• Hammer or rubber mallet
• Pliers
• Combination square

1 **Applying adhesive**
Follow the manufacturer's instructions to mix the adhesive. Select a trowel with the recommended notch size; this determines the thickness of the adhesive. To check that you have the right-size trowel, test the coverage on one tile. Press the tile onto the adhesive and pull it off; bare spots mean that the notches are too small. If adhesive oozes out, then the notches are too big.

Dip your trowel into the adhesive and apply a thin layer with the flat side; apply a second layer with the notched side. The instructions will tell you the open time of the adhesive—how long you have to work before the adhesive begins to set. Don't apply more adhesive than you can tile in about 15 minutes. If a skin appears on the surface of the adhesive, scrape off the adhesive and apply a new layer.

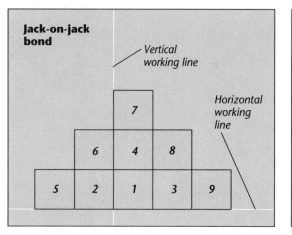

Jack-on-jack bond

Vertical working line

Horizontal working line

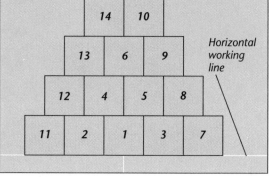

Running bond

Vertical working line

Horizontal working line

2 **Setting the first tile**
For jack-on-jack bond *(above, left)*, set the first tile on the batten with one side aligned exactly with the vertical line. If you want a running bond

(above, right), center the first tile on the vertical line. Press the tile firmly into the adhesive. Don't slide it; this will push adhesive into the joints.

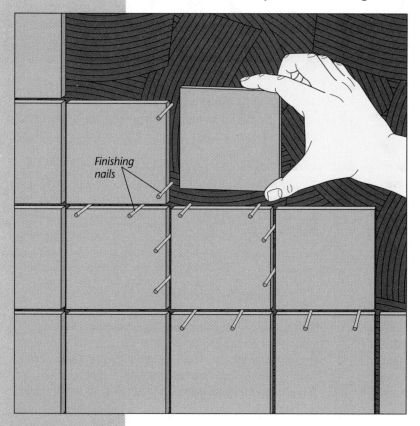

Finishing nails

3 **Continuing the pattern**
Set the succeeding tiles in the same manner, following one of the sequences illustrated in step 2. Use a spacer near each end and both sides of the tile as you work. Just stick the plastic spacer in the joint as you would for floor tiles *(page 30)*; the adhesive will hold it. If you don't have spacers, use some appropriately sized finishing nails *(left)*. Regularly check the tile alignment with a carpenter's square.

After laying several tiles, bed them in by hammering lightly on a piece of plywood large enough to cover several tiles at once; you can also use a rubber mallet. When you reach the ends of each row, cut the tiles to fit. (Turn to page 27 for instructions on marking and cutting tile.) For the last course of tile wainscoting, use bullnose tiles for a finished effect. When tiling to the ceiling, cut the last course to fit, if necessary. Clean off adhesive as you go.

4 ▶ Finishing corners and around windows

Corners require special attention. The tiles in an inside corner butt against each other. On outside corners, set one column of tile with bullnose tiles to cover the unfinished edges of the field tiles on the adjoining wall, as shown. Windows without casings may also pose trim problems. If one of your walls contains such a window, finish off the sides and sill with bullnose tiles cut to fit. If the window has a casing, just take the tile to the casing, leaving space for a flexible joint.

Anywhere that two planes meet, you should leave 1/4" for a flexible joint.

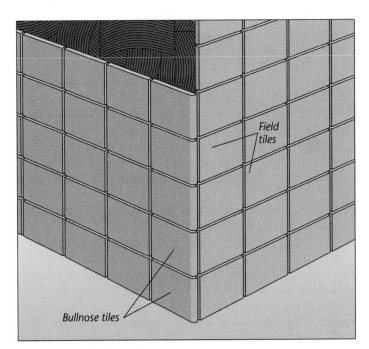

Field tiles

Bullnose tiles

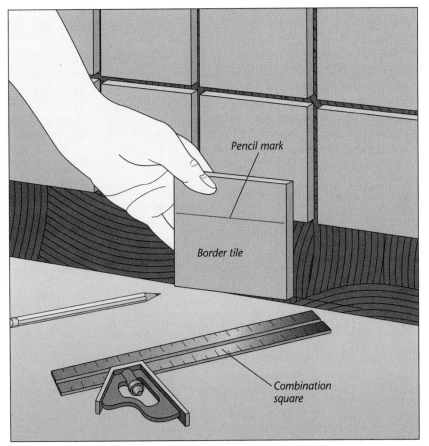

Pencil mark

Border tile

Combination square

5 ◀ Fitting border tiles

After the adhesive has set, carefully remove the wood battens and the spacers. If you used nails, pull them out with pliers, twisting as you pull. Now you can set tiles along the bottom of the wall. If the floor was seriously off-level, you may have to cut some tiles. Mark the tiles to fit, using a combination square. Leave the width of a grout joint next to the floor. To cut tile, see page 28. Spread adhesive on the bare wall and set the tiles in place with the cut end down. Use spacers to keep these tiles from sliding down. Bed the border tiles as explained in step 3.

6 Finishing the project

After the adhesive has dried, install any flush-mounted accessories with the same adhesive. Tape these in place while they dry.

Clean any remaining adhesive from the face of the tiles and from the joints. The next step is grouting the joints; for instructions, turn to page 53. Apply flexible silicone rubber caulk in the joints between planes—for example, at floors, ceilings and corners. Seal the grout and tiles, if necessary.

TUBS AND SHOWERS

If you're tiling your whole bathroom, begin with the tub or shower enclosure first because it involves the most cuts; then continue with the other walls. Cover the drain and line your tub with cardboard to prevent damage—dropping even a small tool may chip the enamel finish. For both tubs and showers, remove such fixtures as soap dishes, towel bars, and grab bars. Remove handles and escutcheons from the faucets. Protect exposed threads with masking tape.

Wet areas, such as those around a tub or shower, require extra care in surface preparation. If the area is already tiled, check it carefully. Loose or cracked grout means water has probably weakened the bond and the backing. If there are loose tiles, pull them off and examine the backing. Even if a tile is only slightly loose, pull it off. If no water damage is present, glue the tiles back in place with a latex- or polymer-modified thin-set.

If the backing is damaged, or if it is ordinary gypsum wallboard, replace it. Study the information on backings that starts on page 31. When installing new backing, first fasten a moisture barrier of building paper or polyethylene sheeting to the wall studs. The best choice of backing in these areas is cement backerboard, which will not deteriorate when damp. To completely prevent water from penetrating the wall, you can cover the front of the backing with a waterproof membrane,

following the manufacturer's instructions. If you use gypsum wallboard, either buy the water-resistant type, or cover it with a waterproof membrane. For a shower, install a ceiling vent if at all possible. If the backing and old tiles are in good shape, you can tile over them *(page 33)*, but if the old tiles come off easily, you may prefer to remove them.

In the past, bathroom tile was set in cement mortar because it is water-resistant. Today, you can use a latex- or polymer-modified cement-base adhesive and grout *(page 24)*. A penetrating grout sealer will further protect the wall from water penetration, but is not necessary on a vertical surface. Be careful to caulk around accessories when the tiling is finished.

Traditionally, the shower pan (the bottom of the shower) was constructed on the job using cement mortar, a waterproof membrane, and ceramic tile. This type of pan is best left to a professional. However, a variety of prefabricated shower pans are available for those who wish to build their own showers. You'll find instructions for tiling a shower on page 48; the instructions for tiling a tub enclosure that begin on the opposite page will also help you—begin your tile above the shower pan in the same way as above a tub. The illustrations below show the position of backing, tile, and caulk above a tub or shower pan.

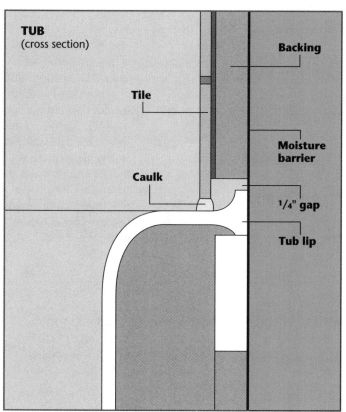

TUB
(cross section)

Backing

Tile

Moisture barrier

Caulk

1/4" gap

Tub lip

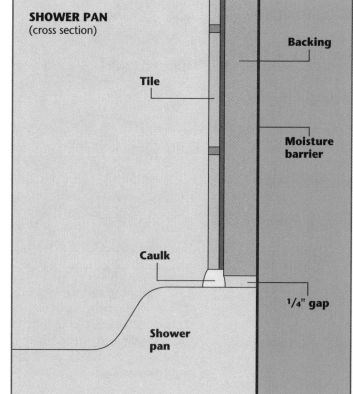

SHOWER PAN
(cross section)

Backing

Tile

Moisture barrier

Caulk

1/4" gap

Shower pan

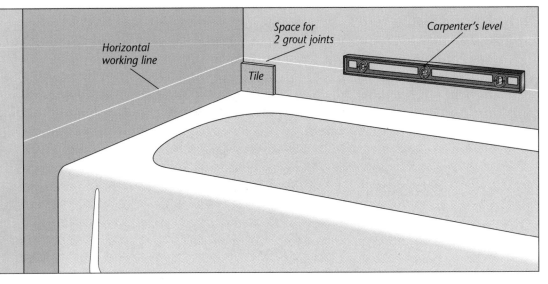

1 Marking horizontal working lines

These lines ensure a level line of tile. There are two ways to establish these lines, depending on whether the tub is level or not. Use a level to find the high point of the tub. With a level and straightedge, compare the difference at the lower end.

If the tub is perfectly level, measure up the height of one tile plus one grout joint. With a level and straightedge, mark a horizontal working line through this point. If the adjoining walls are also to be tiled, extend the horizontal working line to them. This working line will be at the top of the first row of tiles (page 45, step 1, right).

If the tub is not level, locate the horizontal line from the low point; otherwise the gap between the top and the bottom of the tiles will be excessive. Measure up the height of one tile and two grout joints (or stack a tile with two spacers) and draw your horizontal working line through this point (above). The bottom of the second row will be at this line (page 45, step 1, left). You'll have to cut the bottom row of tiles to fit. Nail 1x3 wood battens to the wall with the top edges on the horizontal working lines. You'll start tiling above these battens; they will align your tiles and prevent them from slipping until the adhesive sets.

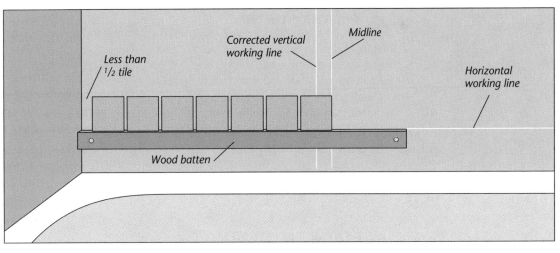

2 Marking a vertical working line on the back wall

To set tile around a tub, you'll start with the back wall. Try to center the tiles so that those at each end are of equal width. To do this, measure and mark the midpoint of the wall on the horizontal working line. Start with the edge of one tile on the center mark. Then, stand a row of loose tiles on the tub or on a wood batten to determine the size of the end tiles (don't forget to allow for the spacers). If the space for the end tiles is larger than half a tile, mark a centered vertical working line on the backing with a level and straightedge.

If the end tile size is less than half a tile, mark the vertical working line one-half tile to one side or the other of the midpoint (above). This will avoid narrow end tiles, which are harder to cut and less attractive than larger ones.

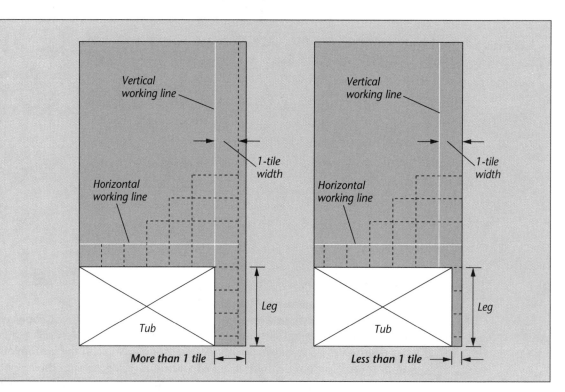

3 Marking the end walls

The end walls are usually laid out after the back wall is covered with tile. If the end wall sticks out more than the width of a tile beyond the front of the tub, use full bullnose tiles down the leg beside the tub; the remaining strip of wall can be left untiled (*above, left*). If you have room for less than a tile on the tub leg, you will have to use cut tiles (*above, right*). If possible, adjust your vertical working lines to locate cut tiles in the corner of the end and back wall. Check your layout by making a dry run. When you're satisfied, mark the vertical lines on both end walls.

4 Marking the top line

Before you spread the adhesive, mark another horizontal line where your tiles will end (unless you're planning to tile up to the ceiling). This top line will guide you as you apply the adhesive and ensure that you won't spread more than necessary. Using a tile stick (*page 30*), mark the top of the last tile row on the vertical lines.

You should make sure to have at least one row of tiles above the shower head. Once you've marked the points on the vertical working lines, extend a horizontal line through them around the tub enclosure. If you're tiling up to the ceiling, include a row of liners (narrow tiles, usually in a contrasting color) to avoid having to cut tiles.

ASK A PRO

HOW DO I MARK THE PLACEMENT OF ACCESSORIES?

Mark the positions of flush-mounted or recessed accessories, such as soap dishes and towel bars, before the adhesive is applied. Don't cover the marks with adhesive. If your accessories were made by the same manufacturer as your tiles, the spaces needed will usually be the same as one or two tiles.

If you're going to need to cut tiles to fit around an object like a soap dish, cut a piece of cardboard the same size and tack it to the wall to show the position of the accessory. As you set the tiles, just omit tiles wherever the accessories are to go. Some recessed soap dishes require openings in the backing. Mark the outline on the backing and cut through the backing when you've tiled up to that point.

To install a grab bar, you'll have to locate and mark the center of the appropriate wall studs with pencil marks on the ceiling before you start tiling. After the tile is installed, locate the studs by following down the wall from the ceiling marks with a level. Screw the bars directly to the studs through holes drilled in the tile.

Tiling the back wall

TOOLKIT
• Notched trowel
• Carpenter's square
• Tape measure
• Carpenter's level
• Rubber mallet or hammer

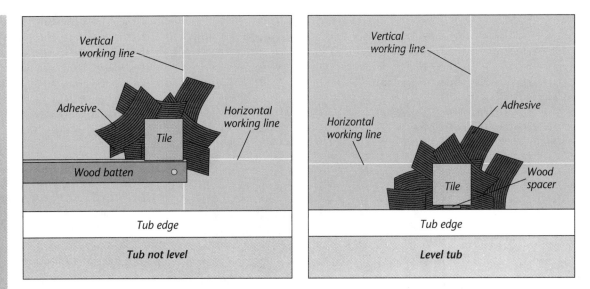

1 Applying adhesive and setting the first tile

Spread adhesive on the back wall with a notched trowel; follow the method described for wall tiles on page 40. Make sure that you leave blank spaces in the marked locations for later installation of accessories *(opposite)*.

If you nailed a batten support to the wall, set the first tile at the intersection of the vertical working line and the batten *(above, left)*. Set the tile firmly but don't slide it. Make sure that the tile is tight against the batten with one edge aligned exactly

with the vertical line. Jack-on-jack is the traditional bond pattern for bathrooms; for instructions on running bond, see page 40.

When you're working without a wood batten *(above, right)*, you should still set the first tile at the intersection of the two working lines, but the top edge is aligned with the horizontal working line. Use a spacer or wood shim between the tub and the bottom of the tile to keep it from sliding. Press firmly to bed the tile in the adhesive.

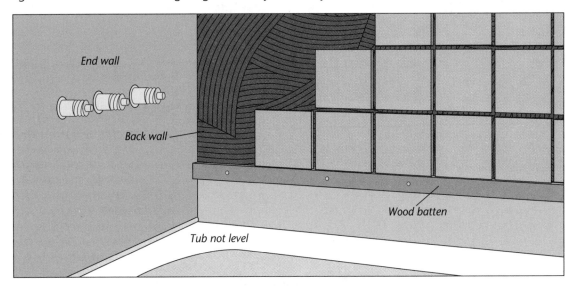

2 Continuing the pattern

Now set a tile on each side of the first tile, with the bottoms on the batten. If the tiles have built-in spacing lugs, make sure they are tight against each other; otherwise use plastic spacers, finishing nails, or a tile stick. Set each tile firmly. If one edge or corner rides up, use your trowel handle to tap it until flush with the adjoining tile.

Set the next tile—the fourth—exactly above the first one, with one edge on the vertical working line.

Continue setting tiles in the sequence shown on page 40, adding spacers as needed. As the pyramid develops in a step pattern *(above)*, make sure that the corners are aligned and check the joints.

As you reach the ends of each row, measure, mark, and cut the end tiles as needed. (Turn to page 27 for instructions on marking and cutting tile.) Check your rows with a carpenter's square and level and adjust any tile that may have slipped out of alignment.

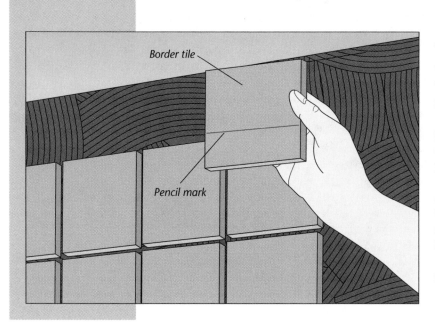

Border tile

Pencil mark

3 Completing the project

If you're tiling only partway up the wall, the last course or row of tiles should be bullnose tiles *(page 22)*. These have one edge rounded and glazed; they may be full- or half-size tiles.

If you're tiling all the way to the ceiling *(left)*, you'll probably have to cut the last row to fit. Measure, mark, and cut these border tiles and set them as you go along *(page 27)*.

After setting the last tile, check your work. Are all the joints aligned? If not, wiggle the offending tiles into position. If any tiles project above their neighbors, bed them in again with a mallet or hammer and block of wood.

Clean any adhesive from the face of the tile and from the joints if filled with adhesive.

Tiling the end walls

TOOLKIT
- Notched trowel
- Rubber mallet or hammer
- Carpenter's square
- Carpenter's level
- Caulking gun

1 Applying adhesive and setting the first tile

Refer to page 40 for instructions on applying adhesive for wall tiles. Place the first tile at the intersection of the vertical working line and the batten. Make sure that the tile is tight against the batten, and that one edge is exactly on the vertical line.

If you're working without a batten, align the top edge of the tile with the horizontal working line and insert shims between the tile's bottom edge and the tub lip to prevent slipping.

For a running bond, you may want to adjust your starting point. Corner tiles of equal width on the adjoining walls give a more pleasing appearance. Check by first making a dry run. In any event, stagger alternate rows by half the width of a tile, as you did on the back wall.

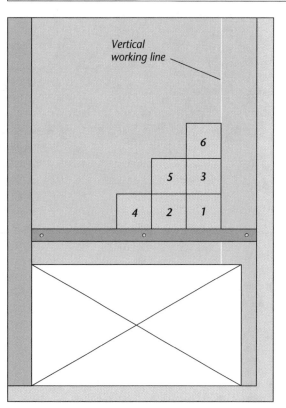

Vertical working line

2 Continuing the pattern

Place the second and third tiles in the sequence shown at left, aligning them with the first. Make sure they're firmly set, and don't forget the spacers if your tiles don't have lugs.

Continue setting tiles, maintaining the step pattern as you work toward the corner. Bed the tiles in as you go, and check alignment frequently, using a level and a square. In the corner, cut tiles to fit as needed. If you're not tiling to the ceiling, set the top row with bullnose tiles to finish it off.

Next, spread your adhesive on the other wall and lay the tiles in a similar manner. The wall with the plumbing fixtures requires more effort because you must cut tiles to fit around the faucet and shower head pipes *(opposite)*.

While waiting for the adhesive to set, check your work and realign any tiles that need it. Carefully clean off any adhesive from the faces of the tile and clean out the joints if needed.

HOW DO I FIT TILES AROUND PIPES?

Mark the center of the pipe on the tile's top edge and cut the tile in two. Then, mark the top and bottom of the pipe on the cut edge of each piece of tile (below, left). Remove the excess with tile nippers and set the pieces in place (below, right).

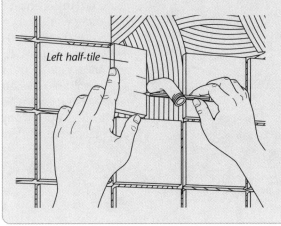

Left half-tile

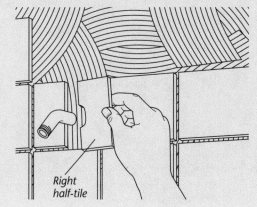

Right half-tile

---

3 **Tiling the border and legs**

After the adhesive sets, carefully remove the wood battens. Spread adhesive between the bottom of the tile and the tub lip. Set tiles in this space; cut them to fit if necessary. When cutting, be sure to maintain the grout space between tiles and tub. Use spacers to keep the border tiles from slipping. Be sure to bed these tiles.

Now you should set the legs (the columns of tiles in front of the tub on either side) and the columns of tiles above them. Depending on the width of the legs, and whether you're planning to tile the rest of the bathroom, the tiles you use may be bullnose tiles, field tiles, or a combination of both.

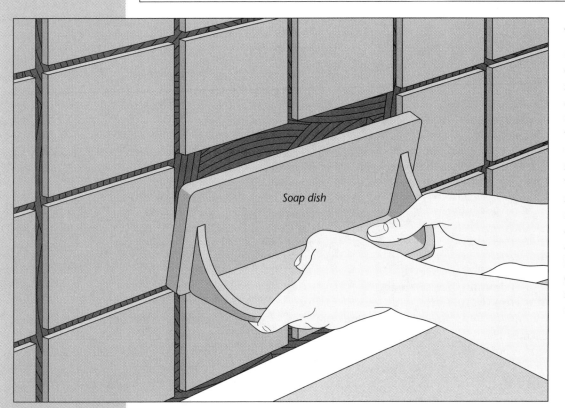

Soap dish

4 **Setting accessories**

If your towel bars, soap dish, and other accessories are also ceramic, and if they are flush-mounted, now is the time to set them *(left)*, using the same adhesive you used for the tile. Tape the accessories in place with masking tape until the adhesive dries. Metal accessories shouldn't be set until you've grouted the joints. (See step 5 for surface-mounted accessories.)

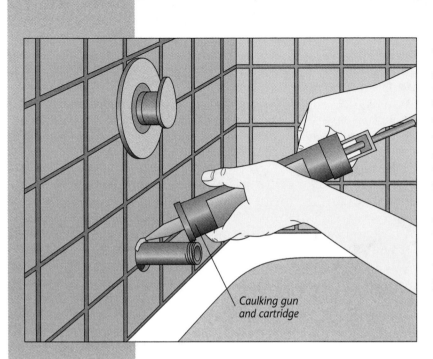

5 Finishing the project

While you're waiting for the adhesive to dry, clean excess adhesive from the tile faces and the joints. Grout the joints as described on page 53. Wait at least two weeks to give the grout enough time to cure completely. Make sure that both the tiles and grout are dry. Then, with silicone rubber caulk, seal the opening between the bottom of the tiles and the tub and between the tiles and the faucets *(left)* and shower head.

If you're using surface-mounted accessories, mark and drill the holes and fasten the accessories with toggle bolts or other appropriate type of anchor. Soap dishes require a bead of caulk applied behind the flange. Wipe off any that squeezes out when you mount the dish.

Caulking gun and cartridge

Tiling a shower

TOOLKIT
- Rubber mallet or hammer
- Tape measure
- Notched trowel
- Carpenter's square
- Carpenter's level
- Caulking gun

1 Laying out and setting the tile

Mark working lines on the back wall and then on the sides. If your shower walls partially enclose the front, use the back corners as your vertical working lines if the back wall is plumb. Any cut tiles will be hidden in the front corners.

Spread adhesive on the back wall as described for walls *(page 40)* and set the tiles as described for tiling a tub enclosure *(page 45)*.

When the back is complete, tile the sides of the shower in the same way. Tile work on the front of an enclosed shower is done last.

NOTE: If you want to tile your ceiling, you should do it before the walls. Support the tile with strips of plywood over each course supported by lengths of 2x4 wedged between the shower pan and the ceiling.

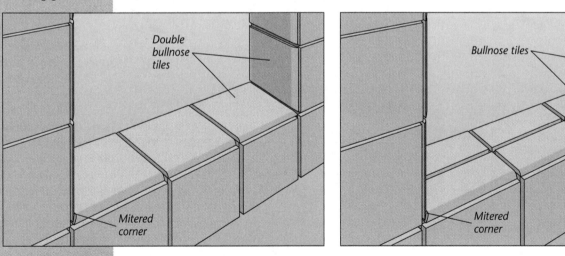

Double bullnose tiles

Mitered corner

Bullnose tiles

Mitered corner

2 Trimming the opening and finishing the project

You can trim the shower opening using double bullnose tiles *(above, left)* or regular bullnose tiles *(above, right)*. Have your dealer cut the mitered corners. Special curb pieces that shed water more effectively than double bullnose tiles are available from some manufacturers.

After the adhesive has dried, carefully grout all the joints between the tiles as explained on page 53. Apply silicone rubber caulk to seal the joints between the shower pan and the tile and around the faucet handles, the shower head, and the soap dish or any other accessories.

SINKS AND COUNTERS

The instructions that follow explain how to tile a sink top; they can be adapted to other projects such as a countertop or buffet.

You can apply new tiles right over existing ceramic tile or laminated plastic counters. Keep in mind that this will raise the height of your counters. The backsplash will be applied to an acceptable wall covering such as gypsum wallboard. If you installed new cabinets or removed the old countertop, you'll be installing a new backing for the counter. For general information on backings, refer to page 31.

By far the most common backing for ceramic tile countertops is 3/4-inch exterior-grade plywood. If you are installing a recessed sink, it's best to cover the plywood with cement backerboard because of the increased risk of water penetration around the sink. Cement backerboard cannot be used flat without plywood support.

Make sure that the plywood countertop is rigid and well supported. For the typical countertop with a width of 24 inches or less, there should be a crossbrace every 36 inches. Where plywood pieces are butted together at the ends, leave about 1/8-inch space to permit expansion. Similarly, there should be about a 1/8-inch gap between the plywood and the back wall. A wood batten temporarily placed underneath will prevent the adhesive from dripping into the cabinets.

For countertops, use a latex- or polymer-modified thinset adhesive. Use an epoxy grout to protect the surface from stains; this type of grout doesn't need to be sealed.

The type of sink that you have influences your project. There are two basic types: recessed, which means the sink is slightly lower than the counter tile; and self-rimming, which means it sits on the tile. Self-rimming sinks are much easier for tiling projects because you tile up to the opening cut in the counter and then just drop your sink in place on a line of caulk. Recessed sinks require careful cutting of numerous trim pieces around the edge between counter tile and sink.

The illustrations at right show methods for trimming along edges and around sinks—your choice will depend on the availability of trim pieces in your pattern as well as on personal preference. The edge trim is commonly one-piece, rounded V-cap. Edge trim can also be two pieces of tile, with the top piece overlapping the tile on the edge. Be sure to leave enough clearance between the edge trim and appliances that pull out, such as a dishwasher. Any overhangs must be firmly braced. A length of 1x2 or 2x2 lumber can be screwed under the edge as backing for the edge trim.

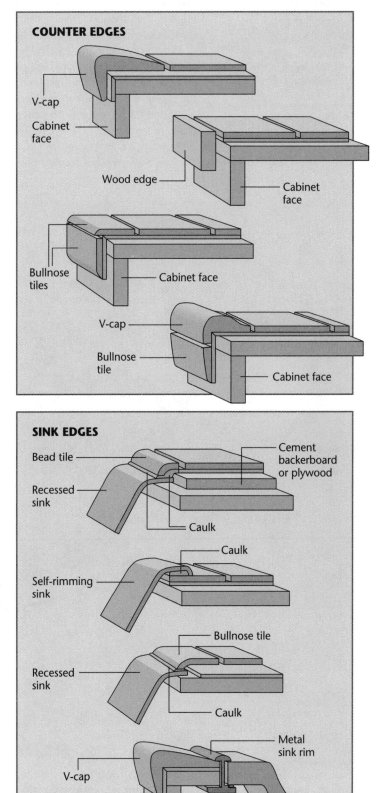

COUNTER EDGES

V-cap
Cabinet face
Wood edge
Cabinet face
Bullnose tiles
Cabinet face
V-cap
Bullnose tile
Cabinet face

SINK EDGES

Bead tile
Cement backerboard or plywood
Recessed sink
Caulk
Caulk
Self-rimming sink
Bullnose tile
Recessed sink
Caulk
Metal sink rim
V-cap
Cabinet face
Sink

Tiling a sink

TOOLKIT
- Tape measure
- Tile stick (optional)
- Notched spreader
- Caulking gun
- Carpenter's square
- Rubber mallet or hammer

1 Planning the layout

If you're installing a sink in a plywood countertop, mark its center point on the front edge of the plywood. If your countertop won't have a sink, mark the midpoint of the top.

Make a dry run with edge and field tiles. If the tiles don't have built-in lugs, use plastic spacers or a tile stick *(page 30)*. Start your layout with full tiles along the front edge so cut tiles will be along the back. Allow for the cove tiles along the back if you're using them for the backsplash. If you're not using coves, leave a small gap (1/8") between the last counter tile and the wall.

Work out from the midpoint so cut tiles will be balanced along both edges. If there is less than half a tile along the edges, move the line over one-half a tile in either direction. Don't tile over the edge of the hole left in the backing for the sink—the tile must be fully supported or it will pull off under the sink's weight.

After arriving at the optimum layout, either mark the locations of key tiles on the backing or set the edge trim before you remove the other tiles. Then you can mark your reference points on the edge trim.

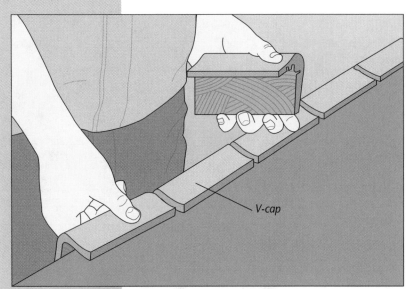

V-cap

2 Setting edge tiles

Set the edge trim *(left)* before you spread the adhesive for the field tiles. The field tiles are generally in line with the edge trim.

If your edge trim consists of two pieces *(page 49)* instead of the one-piece V-cap, set the vertical piece on the front of the counter first. Tape these in place with masking tape until the adhesive sets. Apply adhesive to the back of trim pieces, using a notched spreader, before setting them.

If you're using cove tiles at the bottom of the backsplash, after all the cap trim or other edge trim pieces are in place, set the back cove tiles against the wall. Apply adhesive to the back of each tile and press firmly and evenly into place. Be sure to line the cove tiles up with the edge tiles so the grout lines will run straight between the two.

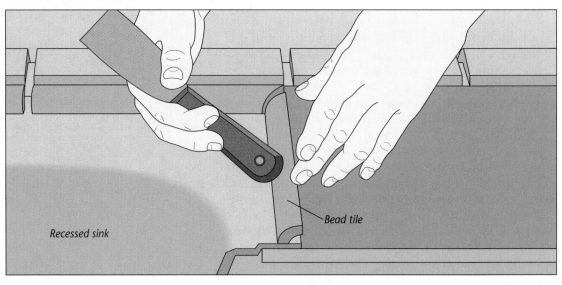

Recessed sink

Bead tile

3 Setting sink trim

A self-rimming sink goes in after all the tile has been set, but a recessed sink should be put in place now. Be sure to caulk between the sink and backing when you set the sink. The next step is to put the trim tile around the sink. Butter each trim piece as you set it and tap it firmly but carefully into place *(above)*. When setting a bead sink trim, use sink corners *(page 22)*, or have your dealer miter the bead tiles as shown. Be sure to line tiles up with any reference marks on the edge trim.

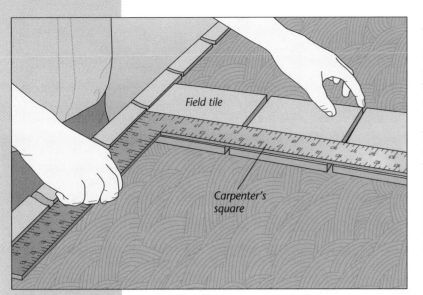

Field tile

Carpenter's square

◀ 4 Setting field tiles

After all the trim pieces are positioned, spread the adhesive over a section of counter, as explained for floor tiles on page 35. Now lay the field tiles, working from the front to the back and cutting back pieces to fit as necessary. If you're not using a back cove, the tiles should run to the wall with a gap of 1/8". Work from the sink toward the ends. If your project has no sink, start laying the field tiles from the center of the counter and work toward the ends. Be sure to use spacers *(page 30)* if the tiles don't have integral spacing lugs. Check the grout joint alignment frequently. To bed and level the tiles, place a piece of plywood over several at a time and tap gently with a mallet or hammer.

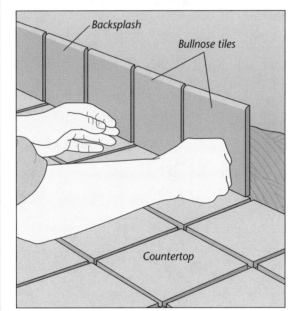

Backsplash

Bullnose tiles

Countertop

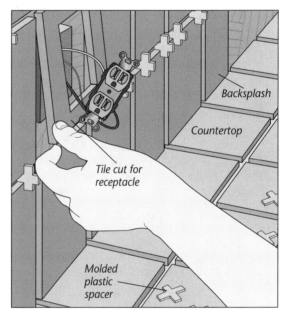

Backsplash

Countertop

Tile cut for receptacle

Molded plastic spacer

5 Tiling the backsplash

If you used cove tiles, continue setting the tiles on the wall to the height desired after covering most of the area with adhesive. Stop the adhesive slightly shy of the top line and spread it on the last row of tiles individually to prevent adhesive showing above the tiled area. Unless you're tiling up to an overhead cabinet or windowsill, use bullnose tiles for the last row. If you didn't use cove tiles for the bottom of the backsplash, start the backsplash with regular field tiles, or with bullnose tiles if there will only be one row *(above, left)*. Space them one grout width above the counter tiles. Make sure the rows are level.

If the wall behind the counter contains electrical outlets or switches, you can stop the backsplash short of them, tile partially around them, or cut a tile (or tiles) to fit over the opening *(above, right)*. Bring the device out flush with the new wall, as explained on page 38.

6 Finishing the project

A windowsill behind a sink can be finished with bullnose tiles or the tile can run up to the sill. Some faucets are mounted on the wall behind the sink. If this is your situation, mark and cut the tiles to fit around the pipes as described on page 47.

Clean any adhesive that might have stuck to the tile faces. After the adhesive has dried for the prescribed time, grout the tiles *(page 53)* using epoxy grout, which doesn't need to be sealed. Once the grout has dried, caulk the joint between the counter and the backsplash.

If you've never installed ceramic tile, you may want to begin with a small project that will improve your skills and give you quick results. Any of the following projects will add a colorful accent to a room.

Whether you're tiling a windowsill or an entire floor, the basic procedures are the same. Be sure to read the section on preparing the surface (page 31) as well as the information on adhesives and grouts (page 24). To learn the techniques of marking and cutting, see page 27; for grouting, see the opposite page. For general instructions on setting tile, refer to the sections on setting floor or wall tiles.

Stair treads and risers: Some tile manufacturers offer a special tile known as step nosing for use on stair treads. If these tiles are not available, you can use bullnose tiles set with the rounded edges toward the front of the step. Another special trim piece called an inside-outside corner (page 22) is ideal for finishing the corners of exposed treads. Follow the same installation procedure that you would for other horizontal surfaces, such as floors, as shown on page 34.

Cover stair risers with field tiles, using the same method you would to tile a wall (page 38). The top edges of the riser tiles will be covered by the tread nosing, as shown in the illustration below, right. If you plan to tile both the treads and the risers, do the risers first.

Windowsills: To tile a windowsill, you can use bullnose tiles; set them with the rounded edges to the front. If the wall below the window is also tiled, the tiles on the sill should overlap the top edges of the wall tiles.

Fireplaces: Tiling the face of a fireplace, as shown below, left, is similar to installing wall tile (page 38). Because of their ability to withstand heat, you can also install tiles around the inside of the fireplace. Depending on the design of your fireplace, you can use bullnose, double bullnose, or regular field tiles for either job.

For tiling a fireplace, always use latex-modified thin-set adhesive. If you're tiling on the inside of the fireplace, check the tile you've selected with your dealer. Tile the hearth as you would a floor (page 34); again, use cement-base adhesives.

Decorative borders: To add a decorative border of tiles around a door or window, fasten tiles directly to the wall with mastic. Use bullnose tiles with the curved edge facing away from the door or window trim.

Tabletop inserts: An excellent use for decorative tiles is to set them in tabletops. Not only decorative, they also serve as built-in spots to set hot pans. Lay out the tiles in the spacing of your choice, but make sure they are lined up and straight. Mark the edges with a fine-tip pen or pencil. Remove the wood with a chisel or router so the tiled surface will be just slightly above the table surface.

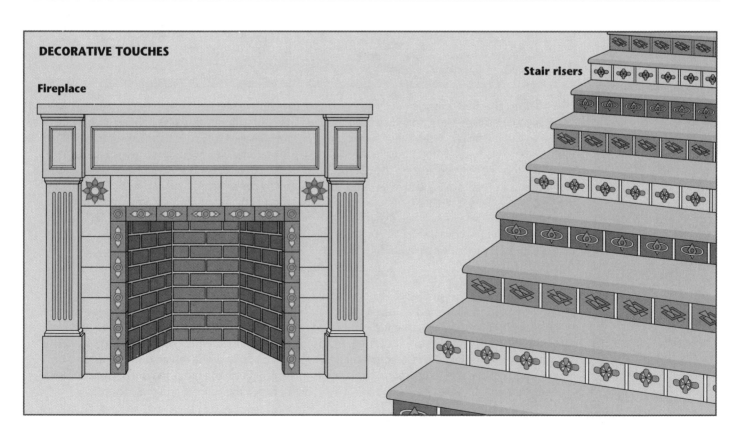

DECORATIVE TOUCHES

Fireplace

Stair risers

GROUTING AND FINISHING

The first step in completing your project is applying grout, which fills joints, bonds tiles together, and adds visual appeal. The final step is sealing the tile and grout. For general information on types of grouts and sealers, refer to page 25.

MIXING AND APPLYING GROUT

Allow the adhesive to set properly before applying grout—24 hours is generally a minimum. While the adhesive is drying, remove any remaining spacers. When the adhesive has dried, clean the tile surface free of any adhesive and scrape adhesive out from between the joints; a shallow grout joint will probably crack.

Properly mixed grout should be the consistency of cookie dough. Follow the manufacturer's instructions for mixing. Apply the grout as explained below. Spreading the grout is relatively simple; it's the proper cleanup that requires careful work. The object is to get the tiles clean without disturbing the grout. Ideally, grout should be just below the tile surface, to show the tile in relief. If the grout is too low, it's difficult to sponge

clean and crumbs and dirt will colle
can irritate the skin; wear rubber glov

If you're applying silicone rubber
the grout is completely dry—about two weeks. This caulk is applied directly to the joints from a tube or cartridge and remains flexible.

SEALING

Absorbent unglazed tile should be sealed. In addition, cement-base grout can be sealed to protect it from stains or to increase its water-resistance.

Follow the manufacturer's instructions for applying tile and grout sealers. On new tile installations, wait at least two weeks before applying the sealer. This will give the grout a chance to cure completely. Both tiles and grout should be completely dry. Sealing tile and grout together is basically just a matter of spreading on the sealer and then wiping off any film. Grout sealer requires more care; some grout sealers will put a shine on tile that can make a floor slippery. You must spread the sealer over the tile and grout and then wipe the tile before it hardens.

Applying grout

TOOLKIT
• Rubber-backed trowel

1 ▶ Spreading the grout
Spread about a cup of grout to familiarize yourself with the process. On counters and floors, pour from the bucket; on walls, scoop the grout up with your rubber-backed trowel. Hold the leading edge of the trowel up at about a 30° angle *(right)* and spread the grout firmly over the tile. Work the trowel back and forth at different angles to the grout to force it into the joints. Be sure to fill the joints so that no voids or air pockets remain.

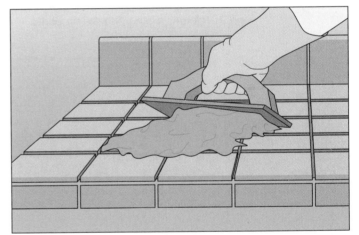

◀ 2 Removing the excess
After this first area, perhaps 5 square feet, has been grouted, scrape off the trowel and go over it again to pick up the excess. This time, hold the trowel at about a 45° angle and work at a diagonal to the joints to minimize disturbance to the grout there *(left)*. Clean your trowel repeatedly in a bucket of water as you work.

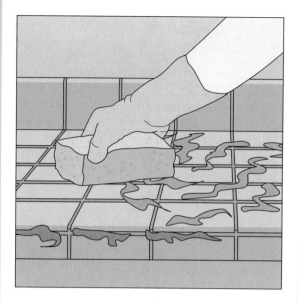

3 Cleaning the tiles

Now comes the tricky part. The layer of grout still on the tile must be cleaned off before it dries. However, you don't want to do it too soon or you'll disturb the grout—the grout must be in the process of firming up. Wipe the tile with a damp sponge at an angle to the grout lines *(left)* and rinse the sponge often. If the grout seems too soft, move on to the next area to be grouted and come back a little later. When the tiles are as clean as you can get them, let the grout dry until a haze appears over the surface of the tile.

4 Polishing the surface

When the grout has hardened, go back and wipe off the haze with soft, clean cloths *(right)*, again without disturbing the grout in the joints. The tiles must be wiped almost individually. After they are all clean, let the grout dry overnight. If grout has ridden up onto the tile in some spots, use the back of an old toothbrush or a small stick wrapped in a cloth to clean along the tile edges.

WORKING WITH MOSAICS

Mosaic sheets have many tiles mounted on a material such as fiberglass mesh. (See page 20 for general information on mosaics.) The requirements for surface preparation and backings are the same as for regular tiles, and you must lay out working lines for mosaics as you would for single tiles.

The basic installation method is the same as that for individual tiles, but you use sheets containing one or two square feet of tile instead of single tiles. Sheets are much faster to install than single tiles, so you'll find you can cover larger areas with adhesive.

As you set the mosaic sheets, you may have to move them about slightly right after laying them in the adhesive to keep the joints straight. Check frequently for alignment. Grouting mosaics is the same as for individual tiles.

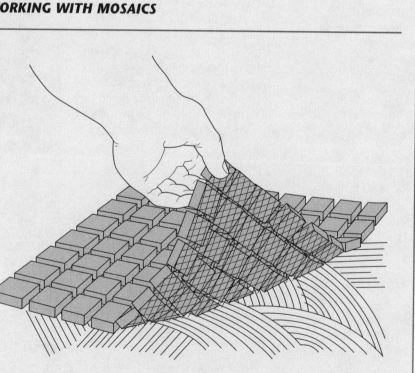

CARE AND REPLACEMENT

Ceramic tile is one of the easiest surfaces to care for and keep clean. If you've used glazed tiles and epoxy grout, your surface should be very stain-resistant. Over time, if individual tiles become loose or damaged, they can easily be replaced.

CLEANING TIPS

Routine cleaning requires only washing with hot water and a mild detergent or all-purpose household cleaner. After washing the tile, rinse it thoroughly to remove detergent film; then wipe dry with a soft, dry cloth. For stubborn dirt, scrub tiles with a household cleansing powder. Don't use a cleaner containing bleach; this can pull the color out of colored grouts. You might also try a tile cleaner available from your dealer or in hardware stores. Read the directions and precautions on the labels of tile cleaners before using them. Some tile cleaners have harsh acids that will etch glazed tiles if left on the surface too long—use them sparingly. Acidic cleaners can also damage grout.

On floors, use a broom or dust mop for removing loose dirt and a damp mop for cleaning. For other surfaces (walls, countertops, and so on), use a sponge or cloth to apply the cleaning solution. For rough scrubbing, use a stiff-bristled scrub brush or nylon scrubbing pad. Avoid using steel wool pads on ceramic tiles—they may cause rust stains.

In addition to routine cleaning, you can keep grout looking new by scrubbing it occasionally with a toothbrush and a household cleaner that does not contain bleach. If your grout is colored, test the cleaner in an inconspicuous place before you use it. It's difficult to predict how the chemicals will react with the pigment in the grout.

DEALING WITH STAINS

If you have hard water, spots and deposits may build up on tiles that are installed in shower enclosures, on sink counters, and in other wet areas. You can help prevent such buildups by keeping the tile surfaces dry. Use a sponge to wipe water off the tiles after showering or doing dishes. To prevent stains, wipe up spills as soon as they happen. Even the hardest tile surface may pick up a stain or two. There are so many t[...] and stains that no simple rules for sta[...] given. The chart on the next page co[...] mon and troublesome stains. If a stain won't come off after one attempt, try again. If the cleaner you are using seems too weak, make it more concentrated. In most cases, using hot water in your cleaning solution will cause it to work faster.

REPLACING GROUT

If grout is cracked, badly worn, or permanently stained, scrape the old grout from the joints with a lever-type can opener or narrow-tip screwdriver. Scrub the joint surfaces clean with an old toothbrush and apply the grout *(page 53)*. Most hardware stores sell grout in small quantities for replacement purposes.

REPLACING TILES

If one of your tiles is damaged, you can replace it by following the instructions for wall tiles on page 56; the steps are the same for floor tiles. If you don't have any tiles left over from the original installation, it may be hard to find an exact match. Check dealers' seconds or put in a decorative tile. When looking for replacements, take a sample of the original tile, if possible. For a loose tile, pry up the tile and scrape all traces of adhesive and grout from the tile. Then follow steps 5 to 9 *(page 57)* to replace the tile.

Several loose tiles indicates a more serious problem. Don't be afraid to pull off a tile that's only a little loose; it will only get worse later on. If the backing seems to be badly damaged, you'll have to replace it. If the backing is gypsum wallboard, you can remove whole sections with the tiles attached by punching holes through the wallboard and then prying it away from the studs using a prybar. If the backing is plywood, first try to remove the tiles one by one. If this doesn't work, remove just those tiles around the edge of the floor and then cut down through the plywood. If you can't get the tiles off, cut through them with a special power saw available from your tile dealer.

SEALING TUBS

As the tub is repeatedly filled and emptied, it will tend to shift under the weight, breaking the seal between the top of the tub and the wall. As shown on page 59, you can renew the seal with silicone rubber caulk or cover it with bead tiles.

PLAY IT SAFE

WORKING WITH CLEANERS
Never mix cleaners containing acid or ammonia with chlorine bleach. The resulting chemical reaction releases the chlorine as a poisonous gas.

n	Cleaner and method
nk, blood, coffee, mustard, fruit juice	Use a nonbleach cleaner and leave on the surface for several minutes; then rinse off.
Motor oil (on quarry tile)	Use a fluid mixture of plaster of paris to draw out the stain. Brush over the surface, let dry for 24 hours, and scrape off with stiff broom; repeat if necessary.
Vegetable oil (on quarry tile)	Scrub with detergent. If that doesn't work, scrub the surface with 10% sodium carbonate (washing soda) solution in water. You can mop with 5% sodium hydroxide (caustic soda) for faster action.
Rust marks	Scrub with nonbleach scouring powder; rinse.
Paint (new stain)	Apply a commercial paint remover, let it stand, and then scrape off the loose paint with a razor blade.
Paint (old stain), dried plaster	Scrape loose paint or plaster off with a razor blade; finish with paint remover.
Hard water stains, soap film, mildew	Use a mildew-removal product.

Replacing a wall tile

TOOLKIT
- Lever-type can opener
- Glass cutter
- Straightedge
- Claw hammer
- Nailset
- Cold chisel
- Ball-peen hammer or hand-drilling hammer
- Putty knife or notched spreader
- Rubber-backed trowel

1 ▶ Removing grout
Use a lever-type can opener to remove grout from the joints around the damaged tile.

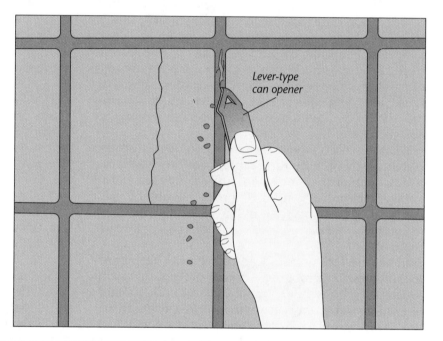

Lever-type can opener

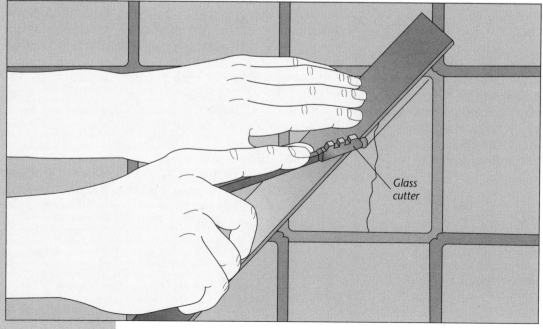

Glass cutter

◀ 2 Scoring the old tile
With a glass cutter, score a deep X across the face of the tile, from corner to corner. Use a straightedge as a guide.

3 ▸ Puncturing the old tile

Punch a hole through the center of the damaged tile with a hammer and nailset or a large nail. Be careful not to damage the surface behind the tile.

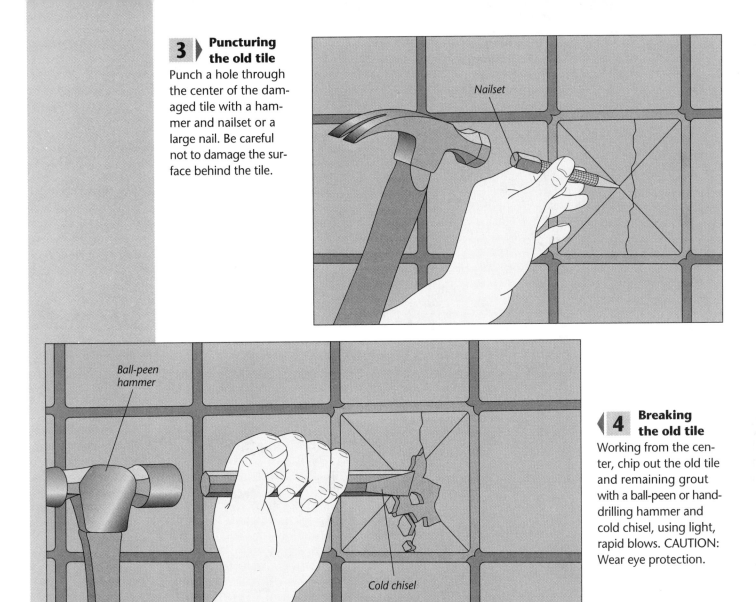

4 ▸ Breaking the old tile

Working from the center, chip out the old tile and remaining grout with a ball-peen or hand-drilling hammer and cold chisel, using light, rapid blows. CAUTION: Wear eye protection.

5 ▸ Cleaning the backing

Wearing eye protection, clean the surface behind the tile with a cold chisel, removing the old adhesive and grout. Smooth rough edges with sandpaper.

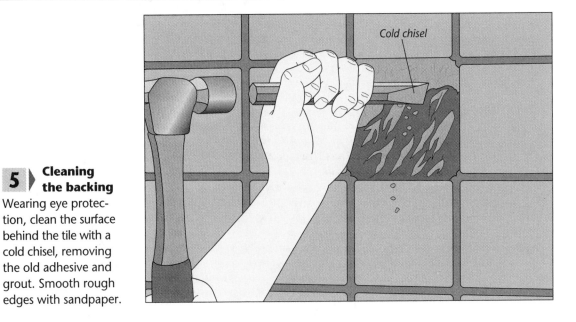

6 ▶ Patching the backing

If the backing is damaged, you'll need to fill and smooth it. Use patching plaster for gypsum wallboard; for concrete, wood, or cement backerboard, use an appropriate cement-base patching compound. Make sure not to overfill.

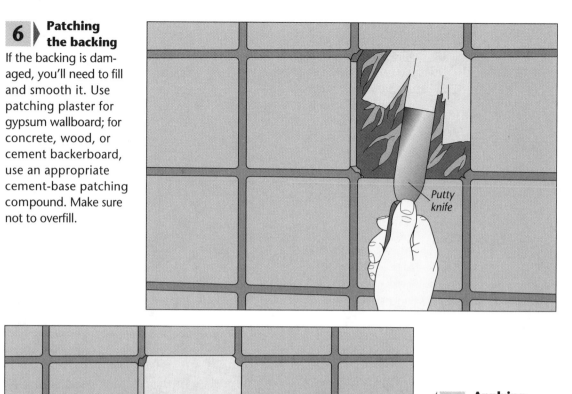

Putty knife

7 ◀ Applying new adhesive

When the patch has dried, apply adhesive to the back of the new tile with a putty knife or notched spreader. Keep the adhesive about 1/2" away from the edge of the tile.

Putty knife

8 ▶ Setting the new tile

Using a hammer and a block of wood, gently tap the new tile until it's level *(right)*. Hold it in place with spacers *(page 30)* and masking tape. Wait 24 hours before grouting.

Rubber-backed trowel

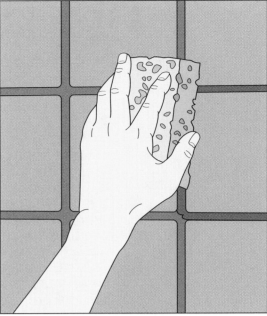

9 Grouting and cleaning

Apply grout with a rubber-backed trowel *(left)*, dragging the trowel diagonally across the tile joints. You can also use a rubber squeegee or putty knife. Clean the face of the tile with a damp sponge *(above)* and then a dry cloth.

Resealing a tub

TOOLKIT
• Lever-type can opener

Applying new caulk
First scrape away the old caulk with a lever-type can opener. Clean and dry the area thoroughly to ensure a good seal. Holding the tube of silicone rubber caulk at a 45° angle, slowly squeeze the caulk into the tub joint, as shown at right, using a steady, continuous motion. If you can do each side of the tub without stopping, the line of caulk will be smoother and neater. Wait at least 24 hours before using the tub.

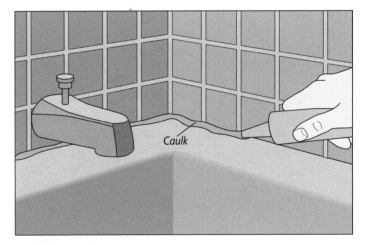

Caulk

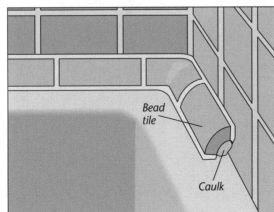

Bead tile

Caulk

Applying edging tiles
If you find the caulked bathtub-wall joint tends to open, apply bead edging tiles (also referred to as quarter-round tiles), as shown at left. Available in kits, the tiles are easy to install around the rim of the tub; use silicone rubber caulk as an adhesive. Be sure to scrape away old caulk (using a lever-type can opener) and clean and dry the area before you begin.

OUTDOOR PAVING

O n the following pages, we'll show you how to lay ceramic tile and other paving units outdoors. Although ceramic tiles most often grace the interior of a home, their durability and beauty makes them eminently suitable for exterior use as well. Extending a tile floor outside to a patio creates a strong visual tie, making both areas appear larger. The other common paving materials—brick and concrete—offer an economical alternative to ceramic tile and are both attractive and durable.

Turn to page 63 for information on the tools and techniques you'll require. We'll show you how to lay tile and brick paving units in wet mortar *(page 64)* and brick and concrete pavers in sand *(page 65)*, as well as how to prepare the base for each. On page 69, you'll find instructions on maintenance and repairs.

In addition to the paving projects covered in this chapter, tile can be used to add simple murals and trims to an outdoor wall. You can highlight your yard by rimming a garden pool with colorful tile or by tiling a fountain and reflecting pool.

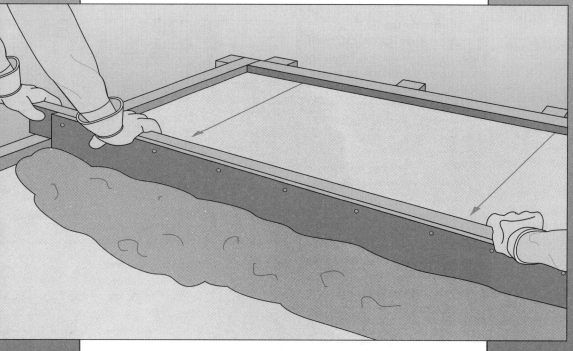

To prevent ceramic tile from cracking outdoors, it must be set over a concrete slab, either in thin-set adhesive or in a thick bed of mortar, as shown above.

MATERIALS

Ceramic tile makes a hard, durable outdoor surface that resists soiling and abrasion. Other materials suitable for outdoor paving include brick and concrete pavers.

PAVING UNITS

Most of the floor tiles used indoors are also appropriate for outdoor use, including quarry tile, pavers, porcelain tile, and Mexican tile. Except for porcelain tile, all outdoor tiles should be sealed to protect them from water penetration and from stains; consult your dealer for an appropriate product.

Unglazed **quarry tiles** are a good choice for outdoor use. Made from extruded clay, they are available in a range of natural clay colors. Quarry tiles resist freezing but are not appropriate for extreme cold. They should be sealed. Similar to quarry tiles, **pavers** are molded rather than extruded before they are fired. These rugged tiles are available in many colors and sizes. Pavers withstand freezing quite well, but they should be sealed. For climates with extremes of cold, **porcelain tiles** are the best choice. These are very dense, vitreous tiles and do not need to be sealed. Porcelain tiles are available in a wide range of colors. Popular in the American Southwest, **Mexican**, or Saltillo, tiles are soft and can be used outdoors if sealed, but only in a climate without freezing temperatures.

The rough surface of brick provides traction, reduces glare, and is cool underfoot. It has a porous surface and must be sealed to keep out water and stains. Ordinary wall bricks often have holes in them; special paving bricks are available without these holes.

Concrete pavers are available in squares or rectangles that resemble brick or tile. They also come in interlocking shapes that form an extremely rigid surface. Compared with tile and brick, concrete pavers are an economical paving material.

MORTAR AND GROUT

If you're using mortar to set your paving units, you can buy premixed type N mortar and simply add water. However, type N mortar includes lime, which will tend to crack in freezing temperatures. If you live in a freezing climate, you'll need to mix your own mortar without lime using portland cement, masonry sand, and water.

Ingredients: Portland cement is available dry in large bags. Masonry sand should be clean, sharp-edged, and free of impurities such as salt, clay, dust, and organic matter. Never use beach sand—its grains are too rounded. Particle size should range evenly from about $1/8$ inch to very fine. Use drinkable water to make mortar; never use salt water or water that is high in acid or alkali content.

Measuring and mixing: The most accurate way to measure ingredients is to weigh them. However, this method is rarely practical, so professional masons usually measure by volume. Once you're ready to begin, you'll probably find it more convenient to measure out your ingredients by the bag, bucket, or shovelful. The key is to be consistent in measuring so that your mortar will be the same from batch to batch.

The best mix for mortar (without lime) to be used for paving is one part portland cement to three parts sand. The amount of water can vary based on the absorption rate of the paving units, and the weather. The final consistency should be smooth and buttery; the mortar should spread easily but not slump. Although mortar can be mixed in an electric mixer, the small amounts that are needed for a paving project are most easily mixed by hand; directions for this procedure are given on page 62.

Grout for paving joints contains portland cement and masonry sand in the same proportion as mortar. The difference is that grout contains more water—just enough to make it pourable.

Curing: Mortar or grout joints should be cured to ensure that the cement and water combine chemically as the mortar hardens. To cure the joints, keep them moist for four days by spraying them periodically or by covering them with a polyethylene sheet.

PLAY IT SAFE

NONSLIP TILES

Outdoor tiles can be a hazard when they are wet. In fact, glazed tiles are too slippery for outdoor use. Even unglazed tiles can be slippery, particularly the very dense porcelain type. Tiles are given a friction coefficient that rates how slippery they are. There are tiles available with a special nonslip surface: some have a finish resembling sandpaper; others have a raised pattern such as diamonds or crosses on the surface. These tiles are mainly intended for commercial use but are worth considering for residential use as well. Consult your tile dealer for more details.

HOW DO I FINISH A MORTAR OR GROUT JOINT?

Mortar or grout joints must be tooled. Tooling compacts the material to strengthen the joint and help water run off it. Joints should be tooled when they are "thumbprint" hard — when they've begun to firm up but still retain a mark when pressed with your finger. To tool joints in paving, drag a convex jointer or a piece of bent pipe along each joint, pressing down (right). Tool all the joints running in one direction, and then those running in the other direction.

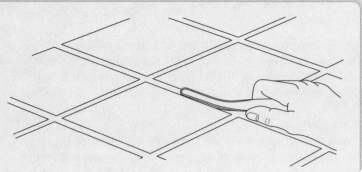

Mixing mortar

TOOLKIT
• Wheelbarrow or mortar box
• Square shovel
• Mortar hoe

Mixing by hand

Small amounts of mortar can be readily mixed by hand in either a wheelbarrow *(right, top)* or a mortar box *(right, bottom)*. Using a mortar hoe, mix the sand and lime well before adding water. Then, hoe the dry ingredients into a pile, make a hole in the top, and add water; mix, then repeat as often as necessary to achieve a buttery consistency.

Another option is the "walk-along" mixer, which streamlines the hand-mixing procedure. In essence, it is like a power mixer—the difference is that you are the motor. Add half the water and half the sand to the mixer, then walk the mixer along to blend them. Add the cement and the rest of the water and sand, and continue to blend until the desired consistency is achieved. You'll need to be able to do this close to your worksite since the loaded mixer is quite heavy; be sure there are no intervening flights of stairs.

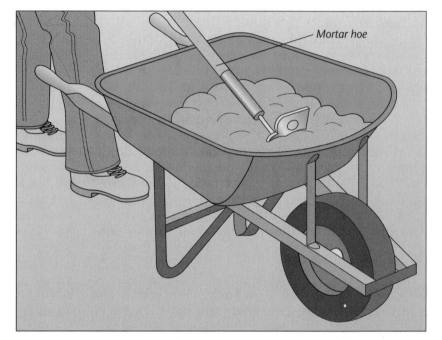

Mortar hoe

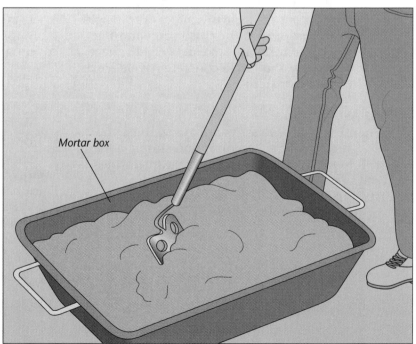

Mortar box

TOOLS AND TECHNIQUES

For paving outdoors, you may need some of the standard tools shown on page 26. In addition, you'll need the more specialized tools illustrated below; the tamper and strikeoff are homemade for the job. For sanded joints, you'll need a bench brush, and, for dry mortar joints, a scrub brush. Most outdoor tile can be cut with a snap tile cutter (*page 27*); for very heavy tile, you may need to rent a wet saw from your dealer. A pointed shovel is best for digging out earth to set your paving; use a square shovel for spreading mortar.

Make sure you have the following safety gear on hand:
• Safety goggles or safety glasses: Wear when using any striking tool, and when working with a material that could splash, such as mortar or grout.
• Work gloves: Wear when working with sharp or rough materials or when in contact with cement or mortar. NOTE: Cement and mortar are irritating to the skin—wear long sleeves.
• Dust mask: Wear when working with dusty materials, such as dry cement or mortar.

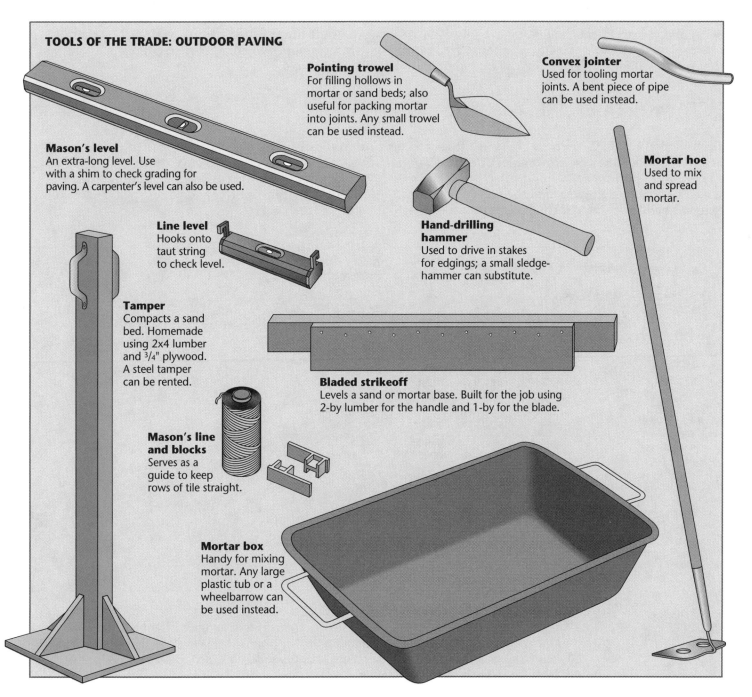

TOOLS OF THE TRADE: OUTDOOR PAVING

Pointing trowel
For filling hollows in mortar or sand beds; also useful for packing mortar into joints. Any small trowel can be used instead.

Convex jointer
Used for tooling mortar joints. A bent piece of pipe can be used instead.

Mason's level
An extra-long level. Use with a shim to check grading for paving. A carpenter's level can also be used.

Mortar hoe
Used to mix and spread mortar.

Line level
Hooks onto taut string to check level.

Hand-drilling hammer
Used to drive in stakes for edgings; a small sledgehammer can substitute.

Tamper
Compacts a sand bed. Homemade using 2x4 lumber and 3/4" plywood. A steel tamper can be rented.

Bladed strikeoff
Levels a sand or mortar base. Built for the job using 2-by lumber for the handle and 1-by for the blade.

Mason's line and blocks
Serves as a guide to keep rows of tile straight.

Mortar box
Handy for mixing mortar. Any large plastic tub or a wheelbarrow can be used instead.

LAYING PAVING UNITS

Ceramic tile must be set over a concrete slab. The instructions below show you how to set tile in a thick bed of mortar. You'll probably need to mix the mortar yourself, as explained on page 61. You can also set outdoor tile using thin-set adhesive; for instructions on this method, refer to the chapter on ceramic tile indoors. Brick can be set in wet mortar in the same way as tile, or in a sand bed with sanded or dry-mortared joints, as explained on page 65. Interlocking concrete pavers should be set in a sand bed with sanded joints only. Other concrete pavers can be set in a sand bed with either sanded or dry-mortared joints.

Paving an area affects its drainage. Unless the area you're paving slopes naturally, you must grade it so that runoff will not collect against a house foundation, or in an area that is already boggy when it rains. You should provide a pitch of at least 1 inch in 10 feet. Generally, the slope should be away from the house. If your project is a long drive or walkway, this pitch may create too much of a drop over the length of the project. Instead, you can slope the project across its width. A professional landscape contractor can help you plan the appropriate drainage.

If your base is a concrete slab, you'll create the pitch by sloping the temporary edgings so the mortar bed will be sloped. If your base is a sand bed, you'll dig out the area to create the pitch, as described on page 65. If you want the finished paving to slope less than the existing ground, you may need to build a retaining wall at the low end.

WET MORTAR BASE

Ceramic tile and brick can both be set in a thick mortar bed over a concrete slab—either an existing one or one that you've cast for the purpose. First, you'll have to stake temporary edgings around the slab—they should extend above the slab the thickness of your paving units plus 1 inch for the mortar bed. The edgings can be left in place or removed once the mortar sets. If the slab doesn't slope, the edgings should slope 1 inch in 10 feet so that the mortar and paving will be sloped to allow for drainage.

Setting units in wet mortar

TOOLKIT
• Hand-drilling hammer or small sledgehammer to drive in stakes
• Mason's hoe or square shovel
• Lumber for bladed strikeoff
• Mason's line
• Rubber mallet
• Mason's level
• Can or pointing trowel
• Convex jointer

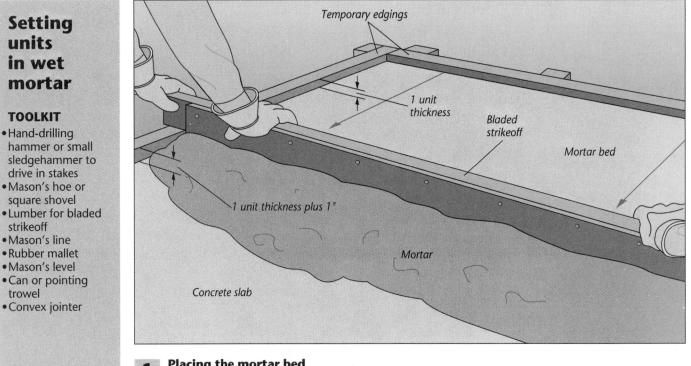

Temporary edgings
1 unit thickness
Bladed strikeoff
Mortar bed
1 unit thickness plus 1"
Mortar
Concrete slab

1 Placing the mortar bed
Mix mortar (page 61) and place a 1" bed over the concrete slab between the temporary edgings, using a mason's hoe or square shovel. Pull a bladed strikeoff along the edgings (above) to level the mortar bed. The width of the blade should equal the thickness of a unit. Constructing sloped edgings will ensure that the mortar bed slopes for drainage.

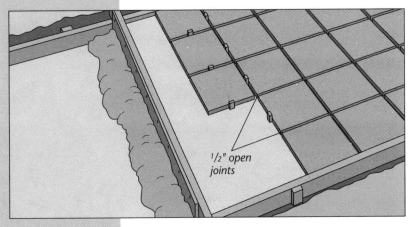

1/2" open joints

2 ▸ Setting the units
Set the tiles or bricks with 1/2" joints. To maintain joint thickness, use wood spacers; you'll need to remove them before the joints are filled. A mason's line wrapped around two loose tiles or bricks is also handy to maintain alignment.

Tap each unit into place with a rubber mallet. Check your work frequently with a mason's level. A shim attached to one end of the level will allow you to check for the right grade.

3 ▸ Grouting the joints
Wait 24 hours after setting the tiles or bricks, then fill the joints with grout that is 1:3 cement-sand *(page 61)*. The grout should be just thin enough to pour. To fill the joints, use a can bent to form a spout *(right)*, cleaning away spills immediately. Or, use mortar and pack the joints with a pointing trowel. Tool the joints as described on page 62. Cure the mortar or grout by keeping it damp for four days; then remove the temporary edgings.

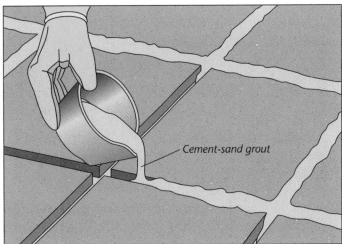

Cement-sand grout

SAND BED

Bricks and concrete pavers can be set in a sand bed. They are laid either with butted joints into which sand is swept, wedging the units in place, or with open joints that are then filled with dry mortar. Interlocking concrete pavers should only be set with sanded joints. To hold your paving firmly in place, you'll need to construct an edging. The first step is digging out the area to be paved to allow for drainage; see the opposite page for information on planning drainage. Then you can install the edgings. The instructions below show you how to build a wood edging—the simplest type. Other types are discussed on page 67. After you've graded the area and built the edgings, you'll lay a bed of sand 2 inches thick and set the units.

Building edgings

TOOLKIT
- Tape measure
- Small sledgehammer or hand-drilling hammer
- Mason's level or line level
- Pointed shovel
- Tamper (optional)
- Hammer
- Saw

1 Grading
To establish the grade, you'll have to set up string lines level with the finished surface of the paving. This should be at or above the existing grade. Create a grid of squares by driving in stakes every 5' or 10'. At the high end, mark the stakes at the height of the finished surface and attach strings at that level. Stretch the strings out to the farthest stake at the low end, leveling the strings with a mason's level or line level (you'll need a helper for this). Then lower the strings at the farthest stake to establish the slope. For example, if the farthest stake is 5' out, lower the line 1/2"; if the stake is 10' out, lower the string 1".

The next step is to excavate below the string lines to a depth that is equal to the thickness of the paving units plus 2" for the sand bed. Leave some earth around each stake to hold it in place. Try to avoid digging deeper than necessary, because undisturbed soil is the most stable base for your paving. If you do create dips, fill them with sand and tamp it down. When you're excavating, dig beyond the edges of the area to be paved to allow for the edgings.

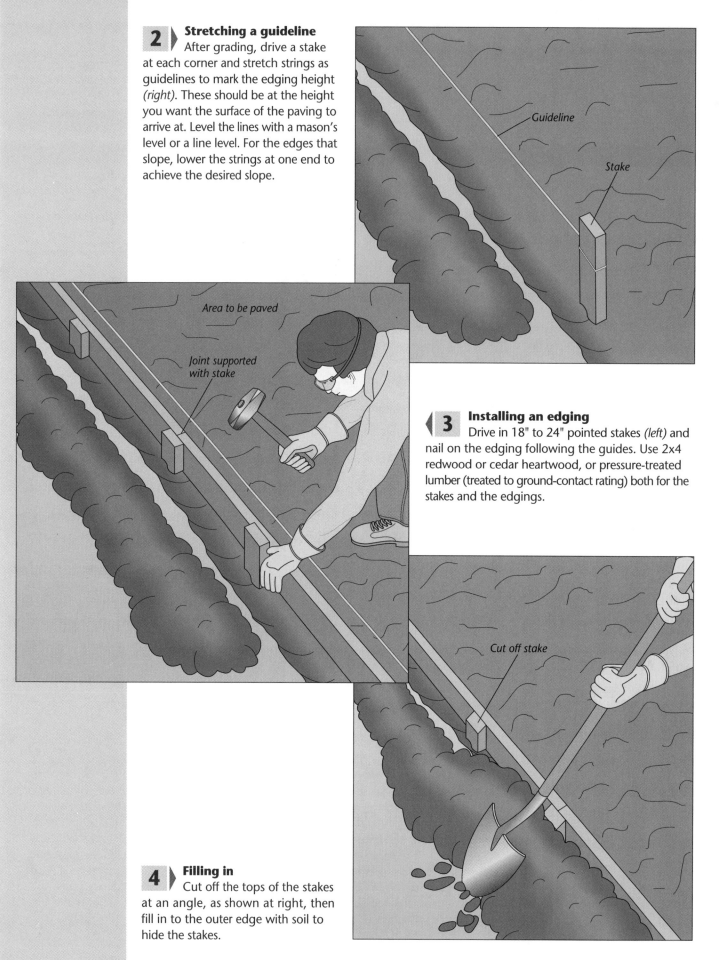

2 ▶ Stretching a guideline
After grading, drive a stake at each corner and stretch strings as guidelines to mark the edging height *(right)*. These should be at the height you want the surface of the paving to arrive at. Level the lines with a mason's level or a line level. For the edges that slope, lower the strings at one end to achieve the desired slope.

Guideline

Stake

Area to be paved

Joint supported with stake

3 ▶ Installing an edging
Drive in 18" to 24" pointed stakes *(left)* and nail on the edging following the guides. Use 2x4 redwood or cedar heartwood, or pressure-treated lumber (treated to ground-contact rating) both for the stakes and the edgings.

Cut off stake

4 ▶ Filling in
Cut off the tops of the stakes at an angle, as shown at right, then fill in to the outer edge with soil to hide the stakes.

![tape measure icon] **ASK A PRO**

WHAT OTHER KINDS OF EDGINGS CAN I BUILD?

You can edge your paving with a row of bricks buried in the earth and set either vertically or on an angle. You can also build a concrete edging, as shown at right. First, you'll need to build a wood form for the concrete. Then, the concrete is placed so its surface is level with the surface of the finished paving.

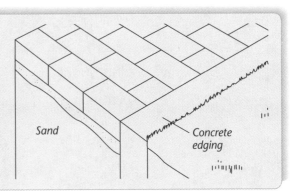

Sand

Concrete edging

Setting units with sanded joints

TOOLKIT
- Tape measure
- Shovel
- Lumber for strikeoff, or bladed strikeoff
- Tamper
- Mason's line
- Rubber mallet (optional)
- Mason's level
- Pointing trowel
- Bench brush

1 ▶ **Striking off the base**

After grading the area to be paved and constructing edgings *(page 65)*, you can begin to lay the sand base.

Set temporary guides inside the edgings, their top surfaces one unit-thickness below the finished grade. If you use 2x4s as shown at right, the sand bed will be about 2" deep. Place dampened sand between the guides, then strike it off smooth, about 3' at a time, with a straight piece of lumber. Tamp the sand, then restrike as necessary.

If your project is narrow enough, you can use a bladed strikeoff, resting on the edgings, instead of using temporary guides.

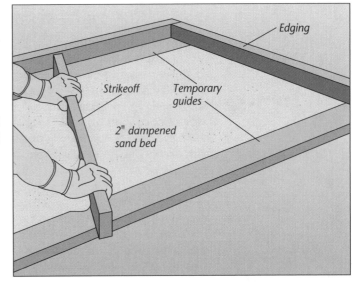

Edging

Strikeoff

Temporary guides

2" dampened sand bed

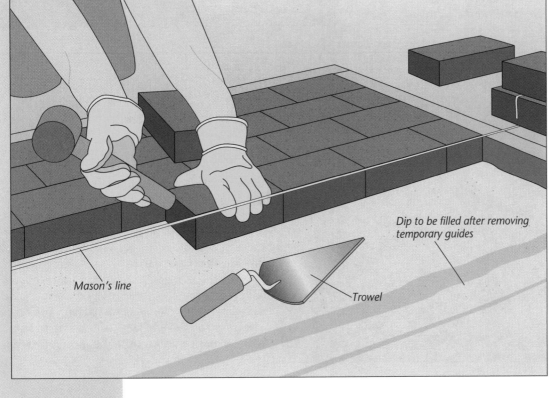

Mason's line

Trowel

Dip to be filled after removing temporary guides

2 ◀ **Laying the units**

Remove temporary guides and use a trowel to fill dips with sand as you go; strike off the area where the guide was with a short board.

Work outward from a corner of the edgings; tap the units into place with a rubber mallet or press them in place by hand. Edges should be butted against each other *(left)*. Use a mason's line to align the units; wrap it around two loose bricks or pavers. Check your paving with a level; attach a shim to one end of it to achieve the right grade.

3 ▶ Sanding the joints
Spread fine sand over the surface of the finished paving. Let it dry thoroughly, then sweep it into the joints *(left)*, resanding as necessary to fill them. Use a fine spray to wet the finished paving down; this helps to settle the sand.

Bench brush

Setting units with dry mortar joints

TOOLKIT
- Lumber for bladed strikeoff
- Tape measure
- Tamper
- Mason's line
- Rubber mallet (optional)
- Mason's level
- Scrub brush
- Broom
- Convex jointer

1 ▶ Placing the units and mortar
For dry-mortared pavings, first strike off and tamp a sand bed *(step 1, previous page)*. Set the bricks or pavers with 1/2" open joints (use a 1/2" thick board as a spacer). Tap them in place with a rubber mallet or press them in place by hand. Use a mason's line wrapped around two loose bricks or pavers for alignment and a mason's level with a shim to check the grade.

Mix dry cement and sand in a 1:3 ratio and spread it over the surface, brushing it into the open joints *(right)*. If necessary, kneel on a board to avoid disturbing the paving. Then, sweep the mortar off the surface.

Scrub brush

Mortar

Wooden tamper

2 ▶ Tamping and wetting the mortar
Use a 1/2" thick board to tamp the dry mix firmly into the joints *(left)*. Carefully sweep and dust the unit faces before proceeding further; any mix that remains may leave stains (although some staining is usually unavoidable). Wet down the paving using an extremely fine spray, so as not to splash mortar out of the joints. Don't allow pools to form, and try not to wash away any of the mortar. Over the next two to three hours, wet the paving periodically, keeping it damp.

When the mortar is firm but can still be dented with your finger, tool the joints by drawing a convex jointer across them *(page 62)*. After a few hours, you can scrub the unit faces with burlap to help remove mortar stains. Cure the mortar by keeping it damp for four days.

CARE AND REPLACEMENT

With the exception of porcelain tile, all outdoor tile should be sealed to protect it from the effects of the weather. Brick should also be sealed. In addition, special outdoor waxes are available that bring out the color of the paving; such waxes need to be reapplied periodically.

Outdoor paving can be cleaned in the same way as described for indoor tile on page 56. There are grout-film removers available; these products are nonacidic and will not damage the units.

Paving units set in sand are easiest to maintain and repair. You can keep down weeds in the joints with a contact weed killer. If a unit is pushed out of place by tree roots or freezing weather, it can be easily reset. Broken units can simply be pried up and replaced.

Mortar or grout joints are trickier to repair. The old mortar or grout may crack; it can be replaced as explained below. A cracked tile or brick set in a mortar bed must be broken up before a new one can be put in place.

Replacing cracked mortar or grout

TOOLKIT
- Cold chisel
- Ball-peen hammer or hand-drilling hammer
- Old paintbrush
- Convex jointer

Chipping out the old material
Fresh mortar or grout will not adhere to old. Wearing eye protection, chisel out the cracked and crumbling material with a narrow-blade cold chisel and a ball-peen hammer (right); you can also use a hand-drilling hammer if you tap lightly. Thoroughly brush and blow out the joints, using an old paintbrush.

Fill the joints with fresh mortar or grout as explained on page 65. Then tool and cure the new joints.

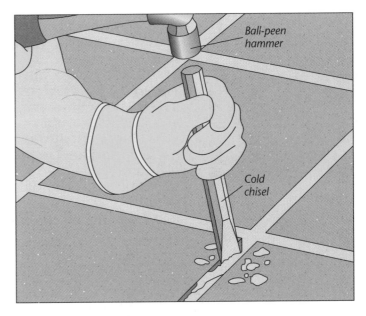

Ball-peen hammer

Cold chisel

Replacing a unit

TOOLKIT
- Glass cutter for tile
- Cold chisel
- Ball-peen hammer (optional)
- Hand-drilling hammer
- Old paintbrush
- Pointing trowel
- Rubber mallet to set unit
- Convex jointer

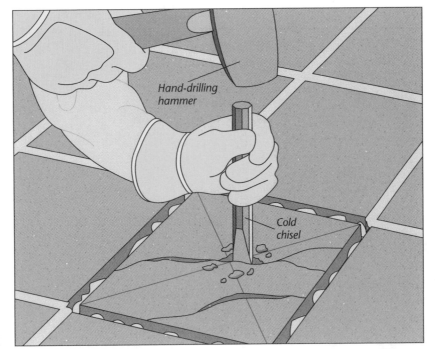

Hand-drilling hammer

Cold chisel

Removing the unit and applying new mortar
Wearing eye protection, first chip away the old mortar or grout as described above. If you're removing a tile, score it first with a glass cutter, as shown on page 56. Break up the damaged tile or brick with a cold chisel and hand-drilling hammer (left). Chip away all the old mortar beneath the brick or tile. Apply new mortar to the cavity and set in the new unit. Grout the joints and tool and cure them.

RESILIENT TILE

Traditional or contemporary, simulated brick or marble, textured or smooth, resilient tile offers a wide variety of look-alikes and a wealth of original designs. A new resilient tile floor can now easily take on the sophisticated appearance of Italian marble, elegant slate, or Spanish tile; or be brightened by a wild, colorful, graphic design. These individual tiles, usually 12 by 12 inches, are commonly made of a vinyl composition or solid vinyl.

Compared to many other floorings, resilient tiles are economical and easy to install and maintain. Installation requires only some basic skills, patience, and a few simple tools. Some resilient tiles are also suitable for walls; however, they are not recommended for countertops because they're easily damaged by sharp objects.

On page 72, you'll find an inventory of the tools you might need to install resilient tile. Starting on page 73, you'll learn how to prepare your floor for your new tile. Beginning on page 75, you'll find out how to install resilient tile on both floors and walls. The method that is described deals with applying adhesive, but the layout instructions are applicable both for tile that requires adhesive and the self-stick type. For tips on caring for your new resilient tile floor, turn to page 80, where you'll also find repair instructions. With your new-found knowledge and expertise, you'll enjoy your new tile floor for years to come.

In this chapter, one of the techniques you'll learn is to properly apply adhesive to ensure a strong bond for your new tile.

MATERIALS

When shopping for resilient tile, you'll find a wide selection of designs, colors, textures, and new materials. At one time, these tiles were commonly made of asphalt or vinyl-asbestos. Now tiles intended for residential use are generally made of solid vinyl or vinyl composition, although cork and rubber are sometimes used. Because of the health hazards, products containing asbestos are no longer sold.

Vinyl composition and solid vinyl tiles are virtually waterproof and are highly resistant to wear, dirt, and indentation. They are installed with adhesives or simply stuck directly to the floor (if they are the self-stick type). Most of these resilient tiles come with a no-wax finish to make cleaning easy.

Some variations of vinyl tiles include fabric, hardwood veneers, or marble chips. These materials are suspended in solid vinyl or laminated between a base and a tough vinyl surface. There are also tiles made especially for walls.

Once you've decided on resilient tile, you'll want to choose a design, color, and texture to complement your room decor. Consider the following points when making your choice: Does the tile have the color and pattern printed on it or is it inlaid, meaning it's continuous to the tile backing? Inlaid tile is more expensive but the color and pattern will not wear off.

Vinyl composition tiles are less likely to become scratched than solid vinyl tiles. Embossed tiles are finished with a grained or fissured surface. Embossing helps hide wear marks and indentations left by furniture, but deeply embossed tiles can collect dirt. Solid colors, especially black and white, tend to show dirt more than marbled or patterned tiles. Hold different tiles to the light to compare the quality of the color and the depth it appears to have. Ask if a warranty comes with the tile. Some manufacturers offer lifetime warranties against the color or pattern wearing off.

Sizes and shapes other than the standard 12-inch-square are available, but they often must be ordered specially. To determine the amount of tile that you'll need, find the area (in feet) of the floor by multiplying the overall length of the room by its width. Deduct the area of any protrusions into the room, such as a kitchen counter or a bathtub. For a room with an odd shape, such as an L-shaped room, divide the floor area into rectangles. Then measure each and add the areas together. Once you have found the total area, add 5% so that you'll have enough extra tiles for cutting, waste, and later repairs.

Resilient tile comes in boxes that contain enough to cover 45 square feet. To determine the number of boxes that you'll need, divide the overall floor area (including the 5% extra) by 45. Unless the tiles must be ordered specially, most tile dealers will break a box so they can sell you the exact number of tiles you want. Check the boxes for color consistency.

When buying the tile, discuss with the dealer the type you want and the surface on which you plan to put it. At the same time, select an adhesive compatible with the type of tile you're using (vinyl or vinyl composition), unless you're installing self-stick tiles. Generally, resilient tile requires a latex adhesive. You should use a notched trowel to spread the adhesive.

Refer to the section on preparing the surface *(page 73)*, to determine if you'll need additional tools and materials for preliminary work.

Adding a decorative pattern

Designing a pattern
If your design will use more than one color or pattern, you can estimate how many tiles of each kind you'll need by drawing your design on graph paper.

TOOLS AND TECHNIQUES

Some of the tools needed to install resilient tile are shown at right; you may already have most of the other standard tools required *(page 26)*. To measure and mark the working lines, you'll need a tape measure, carpenter's square, pencil, and chalk line. If you'll be marking lines on walls, you'll also need a carpenter's level.

To cut tiles in straight lines, use a utility knife and square to guide the cut. Curves or angles can be cut with a pair of tin snips.

In addition to cutting corner and border tiles, you may have to make irregular cuts in some of the tiles to fit around doorjambs, pipes, or other obstacles in the room. To cut resilient tiles, score along the mark with a utility knife and snap the tile along the line. For intricate cuts, use a pair of tin snips. The tiles will cut more easily in this case if warmed in sunlight or over a furnace vent. Don't overheat or the tiles may scorch or melt.

To spread the adhesive, you'll need a fine-notched trowel. And to bed vinyl tiles firmly, it's best to use a 150-pound floor roller, although you can press a section of the floor with a rolling pin. For best results with a floor roller, start in the middle of the floor and work outwards; this will prevent bubbles from forming under the tile surface.

Turn to page 26 for information on safety equipment and procedures.

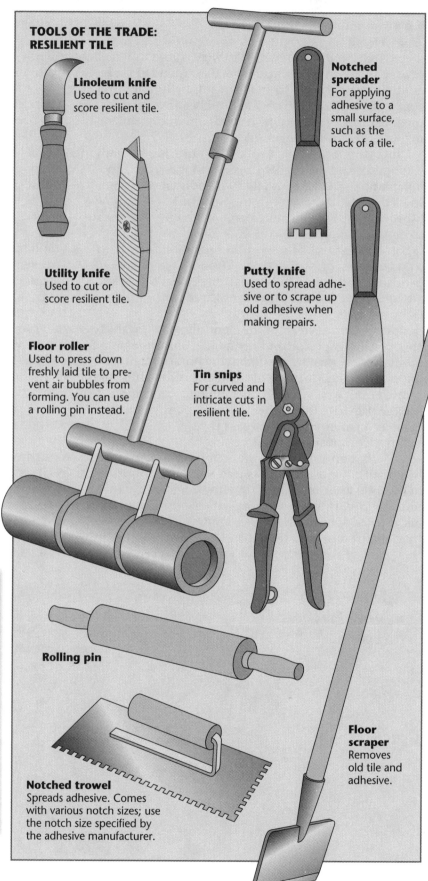

TOOLS OF THE TRADE: RESILIENT TILE

Linoleum knife
Used to cut and score resilient tile.

Notched spreader
For applying adhesive to a small surface, such as the back of a tile.

Utility knife
Used to cut or score resilient tile.

Putty knife
Used to spread adhesive or to scrape up old adhesive when making repairs.

Floor roller
Used to press down freshly laid tile to prevent air bubbles from forming. You can use a rolling pin instead.

Tin snips
For curved and intricate cuts in resilient tile.

Rolling pin

Notched trowel
Spreads adhesive. Comes with various notch sizes; use the notch size specified by the adhesive manufacturer.

Floor scraper
Removes old tile and adhesive.

PLAY IT SAFE

HOW DO I KNOW IF I HAVE EXISTING VINYL-ASBESTOS FLOORING?

CAUTION: Do not sand or tear up the floor if you suspect it may be vinyl-asbestos; instead, cover the floor with ¹/₄-inch plywood. Asbestos contains fibers that can cause serious lung diseases if inhaled. While there is no way to easily identify vinyl-asbestos tile, be wary of any tile manufactured before 1986—the last time asbestos was used in flooring. Old adhesives should also be handled with care as they too may contain asbestos. Contact your local Environmental Protection Agency office or your state health department for recommendations on safe removal.

PREPARING THE SURFACE

The key to a professional-looking job is proper planning and careful work. Resilient tiles don't require grout, but they must be laid tightly against each other in perfectly straight lines.

A suitable subfloor and underlayment are needed on which to lay the tile. You must lay out accurate working lines so tiles along opposite walls will be of comparable size. Finally, you must ensure that the tiles adhere tightly and smoothly to the backing (subfloor, underlayment, or existing flooring). Follow the methods outlined in this section, as well as any instructions provided with the tile.

Remove from the floor everything that isn't nailed down, as well as thresholds (if any), doors that swing into the room, and the baseboards or shoe moldings. If the baseboard has a shoe molding—usually a length of quarter-round molding along the lower edge—only that needs to be removed. If you're planning to put the same shoe molding back after you finish installing the tile, pry it carefully from the wall with a wood chisel, remove the nails, and patch the nail holes in each strip. Number the strips to keep them in order. If you're replacing the wood baseboard with cove base, be careful not to damage the walls as you remove the baseboard.

Resilient tile can be installed over almost any existing surface as long as the surface has been properly prepared. Generally, it must be structurally sound, dry, and free from foreign matter such as grease, wax, dirt, and old finish.

General directions for preparing common floor surfaces for resilient tile are given below. Resilient tile can be laid over floors painted with latex if the paint is in good condition—no peeling, flaking, or chalking. It can be installed over an existing resilient floor if it is smooth (not embossed or textured) and still sticks tightly to the backing; cover cushioned flooring with plywood. All old wax must be removed before the new floor is laid. If your floor doesn't meet these requirements, either remove the existing flooring (keeping in mind the risk of encountering vinyl-asbestos flooring) or cover it with a new backing, generally 1/4-inch exterior-grade plywood. Vinyl floors that are laid with epoxy adhesives are difficult to remove; you should cover these with plywood sheets.

Wood subfloors or wood-finish floors must be smooth and flat. A subfloor of 1x4 tongue-and-groove boards, which is fairly common in older homes, should be covered with a plywood underlayment that is a minimum of 1/4 inch thick; follow the tile manufacturer's guidelines for underlayment thickness. An old and roughly finished floor can be smoothed with a drum sander unless there are nails on the surface; in this case, you'll probably find it's easier to cover the old floor with plywood than to set all the nails.

If your house has a tight crawl space rather than a basement, dampness could work its way up into the house. Wood floors over a crawl space should be protected with a vapor barrier formed by laying plastic sheeting on the ground under the house. Moisture can cause the wood to swell and buckle. Make sure wood floors are dry before laying new tile.

A concrete surface must be smooth, level, and free from dirt, grease, old finishes and sealers, and other foreign matter. More importantly, a concrete floor or wall must be perfectly dry when you install the tile and must not be subject to moisture penetration at any time. This is a common problem with concrete floors cast on grade (directly on the ground) and with concrete floors and walls that are below grade, as in a basement. Before tile installation, test for moisture, preferably during a wet month. Tape some 1-foot-square pieces of plastic to the floor, sealing all edges. After 24 hours, lift them up; if there is moisture underneath, don't install the tile. New concrete slabs should be allowed to cure for at least 90 days before a moisture test is made.

Moisture problems in concrete are difficult to solve. You can lay a sheet of polyethylene on top of the concrete and cover it with a reinforced mortar bed or a high-strength concrete topping and test for moisture again before proceeding; this is a difficult and expensive job. Or, you may need to have a drainage ditch installed around your home; consult a professional. Consider installing ceramic tile instead, as it can be installed over a concrete slab that has too much moisture for resilient tile.

If the floor is usable, remove any oil, paint, sealers, and grease. Clean oil and grease with a chemical garage floor cleaner. Use a cold chisel to chip or scrape off excess foreign material. To remove paint or sealers, sand the floor to bare concrete with a drum sander and No. 4 or 5 open-cut sandpaper. Use a coarse abrasive stone to remove high spots. Scour the floor with a stiff bristle brush and vacuum up loose material. Finally, fill cracks, joints, and low areas with a concrete patching material or a leveling compound. If the floor isn't level, use a leveling compound over the entire area.

Ceramic tile, slate, or masonry floors can also be leveled with a leveling compound.

Wall surfaces must be prepared for tiling in the same general way as floors: They must be clean, dry, and smooth. First remove the baseboards and shoe molding, as well as all the cover plates for electrical switches and outlets. Rough surfaces must be sanded, filled, and smoothed with the recommended patching material or trowel-on underlayment as specified by the tile manufacturer. Existing wallpaper or similar wall coverings must be removed and the subsurface primed with the recommended primer.

Removing old resilient flooring

TOOLKIT

For tiles:
• Floor scraper
• Iron or propane torch (optional)
For sheet flooring:
• Utility knife or linoleum knife
• Floor scraper
• Trowel

Using a floor scraper

CAUTION: Before you begin, read the information about asbestos in flooring materials *(page 72)*. To remove old resilient tiles, use a floor scraper *(right)*. If tiles don't come up easily, use an old iron or a propane torch to soften the adhesive (except epoxy adhesives). Once the tiles are loose, the floor will still be covered with the rough adhesive. Paint on adhesive remover, allow to stand, then scrape up the softened adhesive. If the tiles can't be removed, cover with a sheet of plywood.

To remove resilient sheet flooring, cut it into strips about 6" wide with a utility knife or linoleum knife; be careful not to damage the underlayment. The flooring will come up easily as it separates from the backing, which is still stuck to the floor. Soak this backing in water—don't flood the floor—and use a floor scraper to remove it. When the exposed underlayment is dry, fill low spots or holes with a trowel-on patching material recommended by the tile manufacturer.

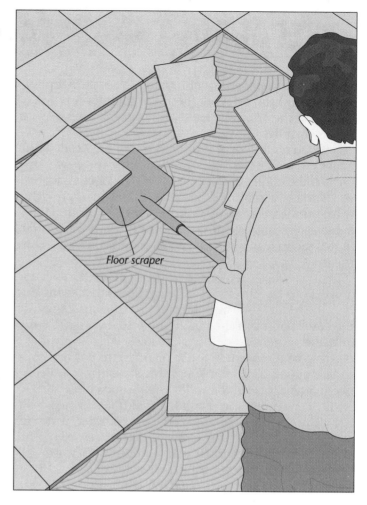

Floor scraper

Repairing the under-layment

TOOLKIT

To patch:
• Putty knife
• Trowel
To replace:
• Nail claw
• Prybar
• Hammer

Patching the underlayment

You may need to make some minor repairs to your underlayment: Fill any cracks or indentations in plywood underlayment with a hard-drying wood filler and smooth with a trowel.

A typical subfloor is $3/4$" thick; this may vary according to local codes. Underlayment thickness varies from $1/4$" to 1". If your present underlayment doesn't meet the required thickness, or is rotted, tear it up (using a nail claw, prybar, and hammer) and install a new one—you can fix any other problems at the same time—or add onto the existing underlayment. The popular combination subfloor/underlayment usually doesn't require additional underlayment.

ASK A PRO

HOW DO I INSTALL NEW UNDERLAYMENT?

Begin by laying the plywood smooth side up, with the face grain across the subfloor panels. Stagger the underlayment joints and offset end and edge joints by at least 2 inches from subfloor joints to avoid hitting the nails in the subfloor. Leave gaps of about $1/32$ inch between the sheets and $1/8$ inch along the walls to permit expansion. Starting at an edge next to a pre-ceding panel, drive nails flush or just below the surface. Nail size and the nailing pattern vary with the thickness of the plywood, so consult your lumber dealer for details.

Adding onto an existing underlayment involves the same procedures: Make sure to offset the side and end joints of the new layer, and use a longer nail to reach through to the subfloor.

LAYING RESILIENT TILE

When you lay resilient tile, temperature is important. All materials should be unpacked and stacked for 24 hours in the room to be covered, so that the floor and the tile will be at the same temperature and humidity. Room temperature should be 65°F or warmer for 24 hours before and after installation.

Three basic operations are involved when laying resilient floor tile: marking the working lines; spreading the adhesive (unless you're using self-stick tiles); and placing the tiles. For each operation, carefully follow the step-by-step procedures outlined below, in conjunction with any instructions that are provided with the tile.

Marking the working lines

TOOLKIT
- Tape measure
- Chalk line
- Carpenter's square

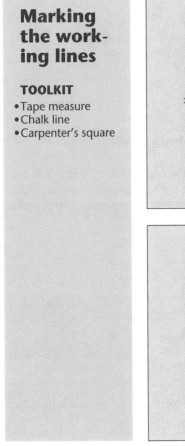

Using the "square" method
To mark the working lines for a square pattern (left), measure and mark the center points of the two longest opposite walls. Disregard any offsets, alcoves, or other breaks in the walls. Snap a chalk line between the two points for the first center line. Follow the same procedure for the other two walls, but check the intersection of the two lines with a carpenter's square before you snap the second line to make sure it's 90° (or, use the 3-4-5 method shown on page 90). If it isn't, check both your measurements again. If the walls are out of line, use the square to adjust the second line until it's square with the first.

Lay a row of loose tiles along one of the lines from the center point to the wall. If the space between the last tile and the wall is less than half a tile, move the center point one-half tile closer to the opposite wall and snap a new chalk line. Repeat with the other line. This will ensure that the border tiles around the perimeter of the room are equal in size and not too narrow.

Using the "diagonal" method
For a diagonal pattern (left), establish the center lines as you would for the square pattern, making sure they intersect at right angles. Next, mark each line at a point 4' from the center. From these points, measure out 4' in each direction perpendicular to the center lines and mark points where these lines intersect, as shown in the drawing. Snap chalk lines across these points to get diagonal working lines. If your measurements are accurate, the diagonal lines will intersect at 90° exactly at the center point. If they don't, check your measurements.

Setting a square pattern

TOOLKIT
- Notched trowel
- Floor roller or rolling pin

1 ▶ **Spreading adhesive**
Following the application instructions on the label, trowel on a water-base adhesive; the proper trowel size is given on the label (usually a fine-notched trowel is specified). The instructions will also tell you the open time—the amount of time you have to work with the adhesive. Spread it firmly with the notched trowel, which will ensure the proper thickness.

Hold the trowel at a 45° angle to the floor and begin spreading the adhesive near where the working lines intersect (right). Spread the adhesive up to, but not over, the working lines. Don't cover too large an area at one time, or the adhesive may set before you can cover it; start with an area about 3' square.

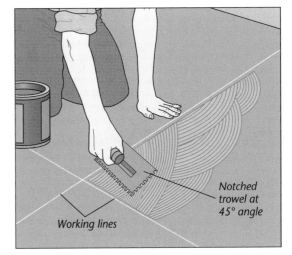

Notched trowel at 45° angle

Working lines

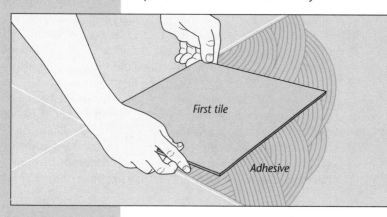

Square pattern—A

				13			
			14	7	12		
		15	6	4	8	11	
	16	5	3	1	2	9	10

Square pattern—B

11				
10	12			
4	9	13		
3	5	8	14	
1	2	6	7	15

2 **Choosing a sequence**
Two methods for laying out a square tile pattern are shown above. You can use either one, although it's best to use the method specified in the instructions that come with your tile. Sequence A *(above, left)* is preferable when the open time of the adhesive allows you to cover a large area at a time.

First tile

Adhesive

3 **Laying the first tile**
Install the first tile in one of the right angles formed by the center lines. It's important that the first run of tiles be laid very carefully along the chalk lines. Fit the subsequent tiles with equal care to keep the lines straight.

4 **Continuing the sequence**
Follow sequence A or B and place each tile tightly against adjacent ones by touching the edges and then lowering it into place. Never slide tiles into position or adhesive will come up through the joints.

Work on the underlayment as long as possible. You'll have to move onto the tiles when you lay them along the wall, after all the full tiles are down. Use 3' square plywood boards under your knees and toes to distribute your weight and to keep the tiles from slipping. Move the boards carefully. Rubber knee pads will make the job more comfortable.

Floor roller

Rolling pin

on the back of the tiles; self-stick tiles should be laid with all the arrows going the same way. Sometimes there are differences in the width of the tiles, so aligning the arrows helps you to keep the joints straight as well as to lay out your pattern.

Once you've laid the tiles, make a final inspection to see that they are smooth, tight, and even. Make sure that no adhesive has seeped through the joints. Remove any excess adhesive from the floor surface with a moist rag. Set the tiles by going over them with a floor roller *(above, left)*. You can use a rolling pin instead *(above, right)*, but it's very difficult to maintain the required pressure. Clean all tools immediately after use.

5 **Bedding the tiles and finishing**
Once the tiles are in position, press them firmly in place. If you're using self-stick tiles, take extra care to position them exactly before you press them into place. They're hard to remove once they're fixed to the floor. Also note the arrows

Laying a diagonal pattern

Setting the tiles
For a diagonal pattern, lay out the tiles as shown at right. The last row that you lay before the border tiles will be diagonal half-tiles. If you're using tiles of contrasting colors, these half-tiles should match the pattern or grain, as shown on page 78. Apply adhesive and set the tiles as you would for a square pattern *(page 75)*.

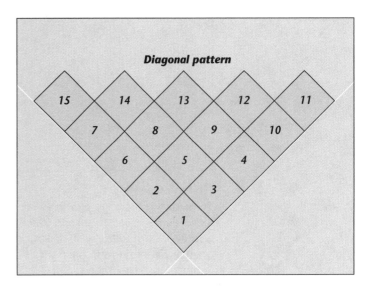

Diagonal pattern

15	14	13	12	11
7	8	9	10
6	5	4
2	3
1

Matching grain or pattern on half-tiles

If the tiles have a pattern or grain running in one direction, cut either right or left half-tiles *(below)* to match the pattern or grain direction of the floor. Depending on how you cut the tiles, you'll end up with either two right or two left half-tiles. If one wall requires left half-tiles, then the opposite wall will also have left half-tiles and the two adjacent walls will have right half-tiles.

Right half-tile

Left half-tile

Left half-tile

Right half-tile

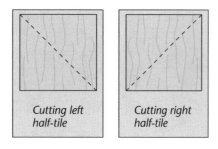

Cutting left half-tile

Cutting right half-tile

Making border tiles

TOOLKIT

For edge tiles:
•Utility knife
•Tin snips

For corner tiles:
•Tin snips
•Contour gauge (optional)

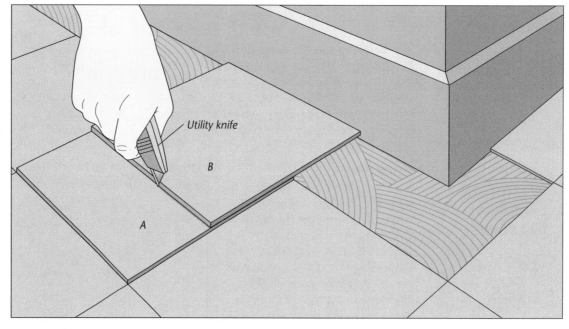

Utility knife

B

A

Fitting edge tiles

To mark and cut edge or border tiles, position a loose tile (A) exactly over one of the tiles in the last row closest to the wall, making sure that the grain or pattern runs in the right direction. Place another loose tile (B) on top of the first one, mak-

ing sure it butts against the wall. Using tile B as a guide, score tile A with a utility knife *(above)*. Or, mark it with a pencil and use a utility knife and straightedge to score it. Snap the tile along the score line; the cut piece will fit in the border.

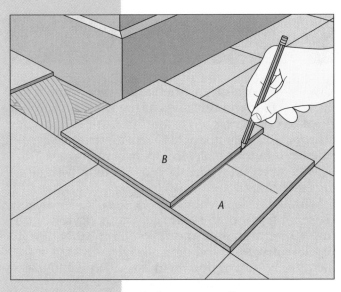

Fitting corner tiles

To cut corner tiles, follow the same procedure for cutting edge tiles *(opposite)*, but do it on both sides of the corner *(above, left)*, and use a pencil to mark the lines rather than a utility knife. You'll end up with an L-shaped tile *(above, right)*.

For irregular areas, such as around a doorjamb, use a contour gauge and transfer the outline to the tile. You can also cut a cardboard pattern to fit the space and trace the pattern onto a tile. Use tin snips to cut the tile to the right shape.

Tiling a wall

TOOLKIT
- Cold chisel and ball-peen hammer
- Carpenter's level
- Carpenter's square

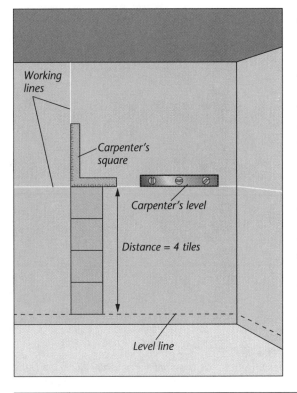

Working lines

Carpenter's square

Carpenter's level

Distance = 4 tiles

Level line

1 Marking working lines

After you've prepared the wall surface *(page 73)* and carefully removed the baseboard and shoe molding with a chisel, check the floor along the wall to see if it's level. If it isn't, find and mark the lowest spot. Then measure up to a point $1/4$" less than the width of the baseboard and draw a level line, as shown at left. From this new point, measure up the wall a distance equal to four tiles to establish the height of your horizontal working line. Draw another level line across the wall through this point. Measure and mark the midpoint of this horizontal line. Using the level, draw the vertical working line through the midpoint. With a carpenter's square, check that the lines intersect at 90°, as shown in the illustration.

To create a better appearance, avoid narrow border tiles at the corners of the walls. Lay a row of loose tiles on the floor from the midpoint to the corner. If the space from the last full tile to the corner is less than one half-tile, move the vertical working line over a distance of one half-tile.

2 Setting the tile

Use a water-base adhesive for the wall surface. You should spread only enough adhesive to install 8 to 10 tiles at a time. When applying the tiles, follow one of the methods shown on page 76 *(steps 2 to 4)* for laying floor tiles. See the preceding instructions for cutting tiles. For a job with a finished look, consider installing metal molding and inside and outside metal corners. These and other types of molding are available where you buy resilient tiles.

CARE AND REPLACEMENT

High-quality vinyl tiles have a no-wax finish that generally requires only damp-mopping. Many manufacturers recommend that you refrain from washing a new floor for at least three days. This gives the adhesive time to cure fully. During this time, you can sweep the floor clean and remove spills with a damp cloth.

No-wax floors can benefit from special cleaners and finishes, especially after a few years of wear. Your dealer will carry products best suited to your particular floor.

To protect the floor from indentation, remove any small metal domes or glides from furniture legs, replacing them with wide glides or furniture cups like those shown in the illustration below. Replace hard, narrow rollers with wide, soft rubber casters.

If your resilient floor is old enough that tiles have become worn in heavy traffic areas, you may have a hard time matching them for replacement. Even if you have some extra tiles stashed away, new and old may differ in color and thickness. If the worn tiles are confined to one area, such as that in front of a kitchen counter, you might be able to replace them by creating a design using a complementary pattern or color. You're usually better off replacing your old floor with new, longer-lasting tiles.

With today's resilient tile floors, wear is a less frequent cause for repair than is damage—cuts, cigarette burns, furniture marks, and so on. You'll probably have to replace a few tiles, and most likely you'll have replacements or be able to find them easily. On the following pages, you'll find several repairs for resilient tiles. CAUTION: Asbestos may be present in tile and adhesive manufactured prior to 1986. Contact your local Environmental Protection Agency or your state health department for recommendations on the safe handling of this material.

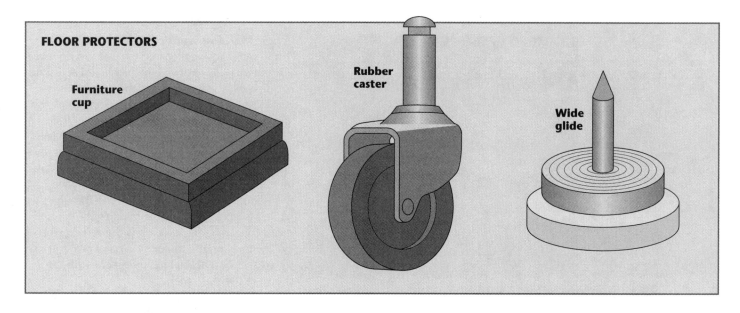

FLOOR PROTECTORS

Furniture cup

Rubber caster

Wide glide

MAINTENANCE TIP

REMOVING STAINS FROM RESILIENT FLOORING

To prevent stains in resilient tile, wipe up spills promptly. Stubborn stains or stains that have set require a bit more work, and even some experimentation. First try to remove the stain by wiping it with a clean white cloth moistened with liquid detergent floor cleaner (use a nylon pad dipped in the detergent for heavy residue).

If detergent doesn't remove the stain, try the following products, one at a time and in order: rubbing alcohol, liquid chlorine bleach, and mineral spirits. Be careful with mineral spirits,

as they are flammable. Apply each product with a clean white cloth, turning the cloth frequently. Don't walk on the treated area for 30 minutes. When the stain is gone, rinse the area with water and let it dry; reapply floor finish, such as vinyl floor polish or wax, if it's normally used.

Avoid using abrasive scouring powders or pads on resilient tiling. Before using any cleaning product, in fact, test it on an inconspicuous area. If you're in doubt about what cleaning product to use, consult your flooring materials dealer.

Resetting nails

TOOLKIT
• Hammer

Tapping down nails
Over time, nails under the flooring may work loose and form bumps on the surface. To reset nails, place a wood block over the bumps and tap it lightly with a hammer to drive the nailheads flush. If this doesn't work, you'll have to remove the floor covering to gain direct access to the nails; set the heads with a nailset.

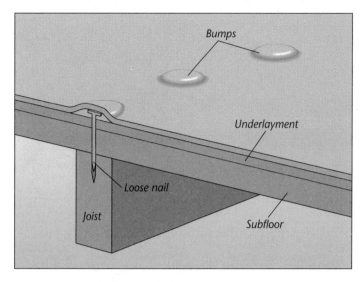

Fastening a curled tile

TOOLKIT
• Iron
• Putty knife
• Notched spreader

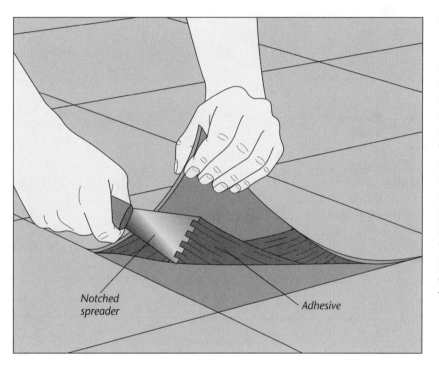

Regluing the tile
Place aluminum foil over the tile. Set a warm iron (medium heat) on the foil to soften the adhesive. Use a putty knife to scrape the adhesive off the underlayment. Then using a notched spreader, apply a small amount of water-base adhesive to the tile. Press down; if adhesive is squeezed up between the tiles, wipe it off immediately with a damp cloth. Finally, weight the tile overnight.

Repairing a bubble

TOOLKIT
• Iron (optional)
• Utility knife and putty knife (optional)

1 ▶ Flattening the bubble
First, place an ice pack on the bubble. If this doesn't reduce the bubble, try heat: either a cloth soaked in hot water or an iron set on medium heat (lay aluminum foil over the tile first).

If this doesn't work, slit the bubble edge to edge with a utility knife so you can apply adhesive underneath.

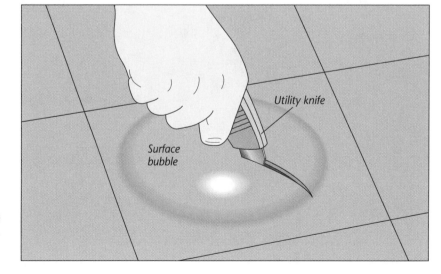

2 ▸ Gluing the bubble

With a putty knife, force water-base adhesive inside the bubble *(left)*, trying to keep adhesive off the two edges of the slit. Wipe off any excess adhesive. Press the tile flat and weight it down overnight, then apply the seam sealer recommended by a tile dealer.

Putty knife

Adhesive

Repairing a small hole

TOOLKIT
- Utility knife
- Putty knife

1 ▸ Making a filler

For a small hole, make a filler composed of fine powder scraped from leftover flooring and a few drops of clear nail polish *(right)*.

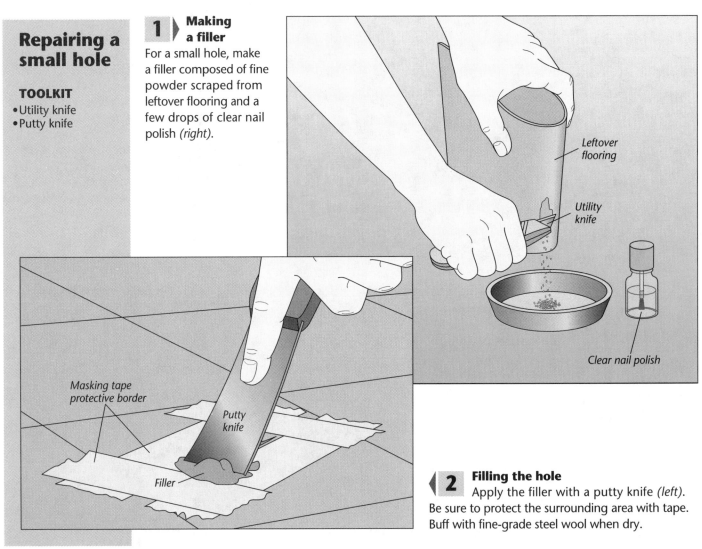

Leftover flooring

Utility knife

Clear nail polish

Masking tape protective border

Putty knife

Filler

2 ◂ Filling the hole

Apply the filler with a putty knife *(left)*. Be sure to protect the surrounding area with tape. Buff with fine-grade steel wool when dry.

CAN SURFACE DAMAGE POINT TO A MORE SERIOUS PROBLEM?

For most resilient tile floors, the cause of surface damage, such as stains, scratches, gouges, or holes, is readily apparent. But some minor surface damage indicates more serious problems.

A regular pattern of indentations that runs for several feet or forms T's (below, left) may be due to separations in the underlayment due to shrinkage of the wood or settling of the structure. If you see signs of this, you'll have to remove the flooring and repair the underlayment.

Small bumps that appear in the surface of the floor may be caused by nails that have worked loose from the under-layment. See page 81 for tips on tapping in loose nails. This may be due to the use of poor-quality nails, nails not driven flush with underlayment panels, or a nail that has reamed a hole in the subfloor. Or, if the original tiles were installed when there was too much moisture in the subfloor, the nails

may have worked loose as the damp wood dried. Movement in the structure can cause the subfloor to separate from the joists, forcing the nails up.

If tiles have curled at the edge or popped loose in one area, you may have a minor plumbing leak (below, right). Stop the leak before you fix the flooring. Moisture in the floors of rooms at or below grade often results from poor drainage outside, a problem you'll have to solve before repairing the flooring. To repair curled tiles, see page 81.

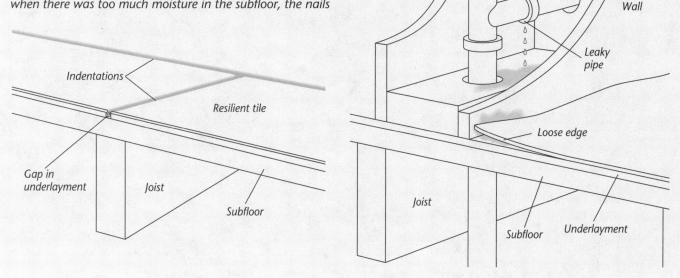

Replacing a tile

TOOLKIT
- Propane torch (with a flame spreader) or iron
- Putty knife or old chisel
- Notched trowel

1 ▷ Softening the old tile

To replace a damaged tile, first warm it and the adhesive underneath using a propane torch fitted with a flame spreader *(right)*. Or, cover the tile with aluminum foil and warm it with an iron set on medium heat.

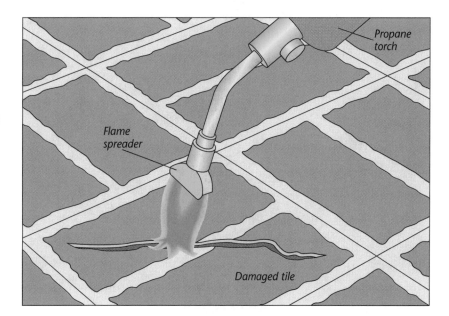

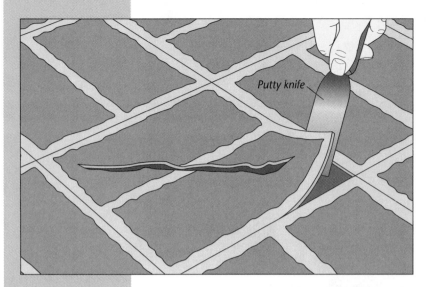

Putty knife

2 ▶ Prying up the tile

Pry up the tile using a putty knife or old chisel *(left)*. In case the tile or adhesive contain asbestos fibers, keep them moist with a spray bottle. With the putty knife or old chisel, remove any excess backing or adhesive from the floor until the surface is smooth and deep enough to install the new tile. NOTE: If the adhesive still covers the floor, without any backing stuck to it, you may be able to reuse the adhesive by heating it with a hair dryer to soften it. Then stick down the tile.

3 ▶ Spreading adhesive

Use a notched trowel to apply the adhesive sparingly *(right)*. Be careful not to get any adhesive on the tops or edges of the surrounding tiles.

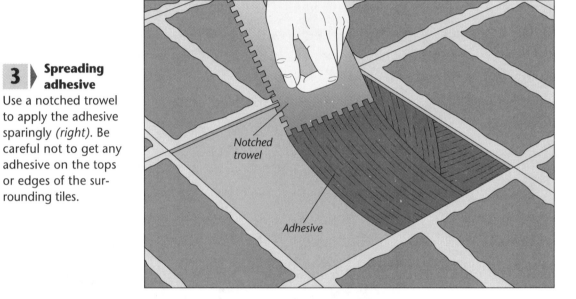

Notched trowel

Adhesive

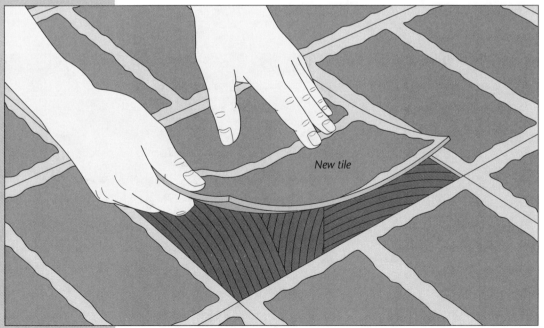

New tile

4 ▶ Sticking down the tile

Drop the new tile into place and press down firmly *(left)*. Wipe off any excess adhesive. Weight the edges of the tile while the adhesive sets.

PARQUET

Floors of wood tiles—known as parquet—once graced only the mansions of the elite. Today, anyone can enjoy the warmth and elegance of these floors at a cost comparable to that of good-quality carpeting. And installing a parquet floor yourself can mean savings of more than half the cost of professional installation. Parquet is available in a number of styles and patterns. You can choose a single style or create a combination.

Visual appeal isn't the only reason for considering parquet. Modern factory-applied finishes are tough and durable. Even if heavy traffic wears through the finish, you can refinish the floor for a fraction of the cost of replacing other flooring materials. Wood is also warm, perhaps second only to carpeting for warmth underfoot. And the actual installation of a parquet floor is as straightforward as putting down a resilient tile floor. You'll find complete instructions for preparing the surface of your floor on page 89, and you'll learn how to lay parquet starting on page 90. Turn to page 88 for information on the tools and techniques that you'll be using. On the next page you'll find useful information on the types of parquet that are available.

Bedding parquet squares into adhesive using a mallet is a vital part of laying a long-lasting parquet floor.

MATERIALS

Manufacturers produce scores of different parquet patterns; some of the more popular ones are illustrated below. Not all patterns are available from every retailer, so you may have to shop around to find a pattern that you like. In addition, you have your choice among a variety of woods, in both prefinished and unfinished squares made of solid or laminated wood.

The cost of parquet is influenced by three factors: the type of wood, the intricacy of the pattern, and whether the squares are prefinished or not.

Parquet is made from many common and exotic hardwoods. You can choose red oak, white oak, maple, ash, walnut, pecan, teak, and other woods. Your choice will depend on personal taste, availability, and cost. Parquet

PARQUET PATTERNS

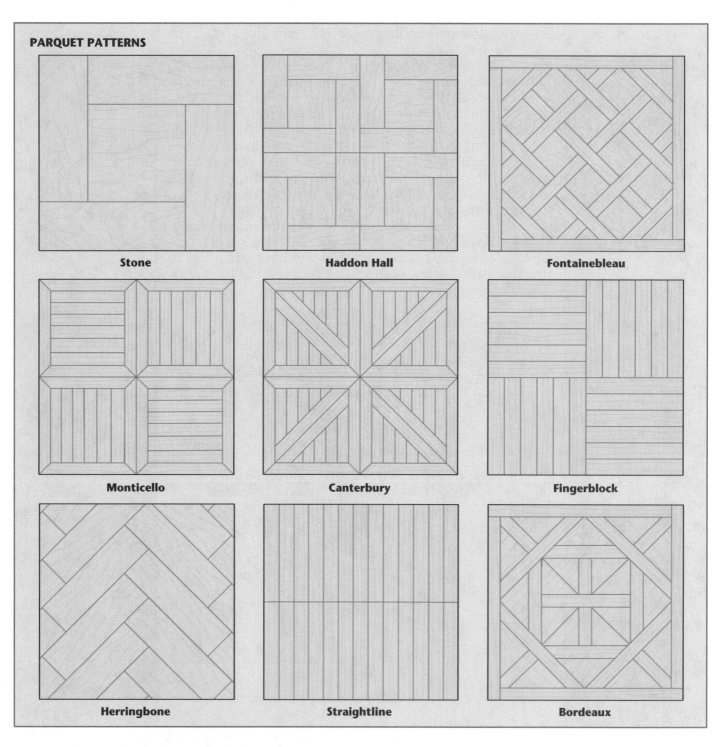

Stone

Haddon Hall

Fontainebleau

Monticello

Canterbury

Fingerblock

Herringbone

Straightline

Bordeaux

is either solid wood or pieces of hardwood laminated together. Both types are available with either square or tongue-and-groove edges, depending on the pattern, thickness, and manufacturer. Both come prefinished, with square or beveled edges.

Solid parquet consists of short lengths of hardwood. This is a higher-quality material than the laminated type. Squares of solid parquet commonly range in size from 4 to 39 inches square, with thicknesses from the fairly standard $5/16$ inch up to $3/4$ inch. They are held together with splines of metal, wood, or plastic.

Most laminated parquet squares *(right, bottom)* are made of thin layers of hardwood pieces glued together. Better-quality laminated parquet has three or more layers of hardwood veneer, with the grain of one layer running perpendicular to the next for greater strength. Prefinished parquet is often precut, so you can readily separate a square into smaller pieces that can fit easily along walls or be made into an intricate border pattern. Fingerblock parquet (also known as mosaic) is made up of pieces bonded to a wood backing or held together with mesh.

The stain and protective coating on prefinished parquet are applied by the manufacturer. The factory finish usually consists of a penetrating sealer that is baked into the wood, with a wax or urethane surface coat for easy maintenance. Putting down prefinished parquet is a simple job.

Unfinished parquet, used by many professional floor installers, is less expensive than prefinished but requires sanding, staining, and one or more coats of protective finish after it's laid; any cracks must be filled. Doing your own work can save you money; however, putting down unfinished parquet and doing the finishing yourself is a tricky, messy job and means the house will be disrupted for several days.

Although smooth parquet floors are frequently a favored choice, some manufacturers offer parquet made from textured wood blocks, which give a more rustic or informal feeling. Once in place, these are sanded until nearly smooth; there's nothing to trip over. Textured blocks are often less expensive than the smoothly finished parquet squares.

To determine the amount of parquet that you'll need, first calculate the total floor area by multiplying the length by the width of the room (in feet). If the room is irregular in shape, divide it into sections, find the area of each section, and add them together. Add 5% to the total so you'll have enough to cover cutting waste and mistakes and some leftovers to replace any damaged tiles. Depending on the size and type of parquet you buy, a box of squares will cover from 10 to 50 square feet.

The dealer will recommend the best type of adhesive and how much will be needed for the parquet that you've chosen. The adhesive is normally a water-base mastic. Solvent-base mastics should be avoided because of the noxious fumes. Self-stick parquet is also available, but it requires a cleaner, smoother surface than parquet applied with adhesive.

As with all wood flooring, parquet squares and their adhesive should be stored in the room that you're going to tile for at least 24 hours prior to use. This will allow the wood and the adhesive to adjust to the room's temperature and moisture conditions.

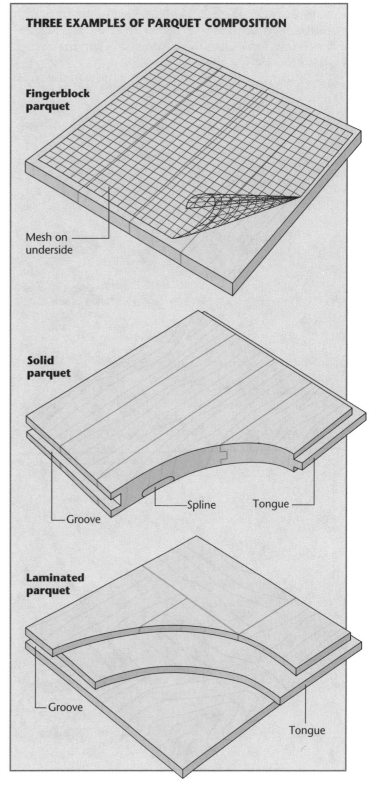

THREE EXAMPLES OF PARQUET COMPOSITION

Fingerblock parquet

Mesh on underside

Solid parquet

Groove — Spline — Tongue

Laminated parquet

Groove

Tongue

TOOLS AND TECHNIQUES

Most of the tools you'll need to install parquet are fairly common: a tape measure, hammer, putty knife, carpenter's square, rubber mallet, chalk line, and coping saw. Refer to page 26 for the standard tools—as well as for safety gear you may need to wear. A contour gauge (page 27) will make it easier to mark outlines on your tile for irregular areas such as around a doorjamb. A pair of rubber knee pads will make your work more comfortable.

The illustration below shows some tools that you'll need to install a parquet floor. A notched trowel is a basic piece of equipment. The label on the adhesive usually states what size notches to use; the standard is a trowel with 1/2-inch-wide teeth and notches that are 1/4 inch deep and 3/4 inch wide.

Unfinished parquet should be bedded in the adhesive with a weighted floor roller, which can be rented. Don't use a floor roller on prefinished parquet; bed the tiles with a rubber mallet. If you're putting down unfinished parquet, you'll have to rent a power drum sander to smooth the floor after it's laid. Edgers for working next to the wall are available; you can also use a belt sander. If you haven't used a drum sander before, practice on a full sheet of old plywood first—it takes a little time to learn how to control one. Never let the sander remain in one spot while in use or it will immediately sand a dip in your floor.

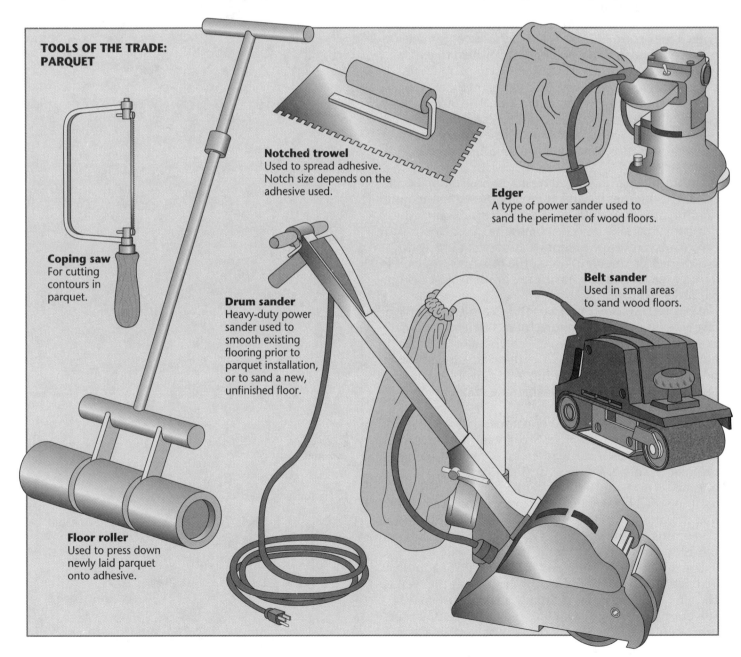

TOOLS OF THE TRADE: PARQUET

Notched trowel
Used to spread adhesive. Notch size depends on the adhesive used.

Edger
A type of power sander used to sand the perimeter of wood floors.

Coping saw
For cutting contours in parquet.

Drum sander
Heavy-duty power sander used to smooth existing flooring prior to parquet installation, or to sand a new, unfinished floor.

Belt sander
Used in small areas to sand wood floors.

Floor roller
Used to press down newly laid parquet onto adhesive.

PREPARING THE SURFACE

You can put parquet down over a wide variety of surfaces, whether old or new, as long as they are sound, clean, smooth, and dry. Note that moisture is a real problem for parquet floors because the wood will swell when damp and start breaking loose. If your house is built with a crawl space rather than a dry basement or slab, cover the ground under the floor with plastic sheeting. Use stones to weight the edges so all ground moisture is trapped under the plastic and doesn't come up through the subfloor. Laminated parquet is the best choice for a surface that is below ground level because of the moisture problem.

The recommended thickness of a plywood or board subfloor on joists spaced 16 inches on center (from the center of one joist to the center of the next one) is generally 3/4 inch under 3/4-inch solid parquet, or 1/2-inch plywood for parquet which is less than 3/4 inch. Check with your flooring manufacturer for specific recommendations. If you need to add to your subfloor to meet the recommended thickness, lay new sheets of plywood perpendicular to the ones beneath. Be sure all plywood subfloor is nailed down well.

Use a straightedge to check that the floor or subfloor is flat, within 1/4 inch over 10 feet. If the floor has significant dips, it may be necessary to install blocks or cleats under the floor or to replace the entire board or panel. With board floors or subfloors, nail down any loose boards and sand any noticeable irregularities. If an existing wood floor is smooth, it will still need to be sanded to roughen the finish so that the adhesive will grip properly

Parquet can be laid down over resilient floors if they are smooth and in good shape. If the resilient floor is several years old, it may be vinyl-asbestos. In this case, do not disturb it; the asbestos particles are a health hazard. For more information, refer to page 72. If the floor is solid and not crumbly, clean it thoroughly to remove any wax and install the parquet right over it. If the old floor is in poor condition, cover it with 1/4-inch plywood and then put down the parquet.

Concrete makes a good subfloor if it's dry, level, and clean. (Concrete is not a suitable backing for self-stick parquet.) Concrete does have the disadvantage of being porous. Parquet should not be laid on a concrete subfloor that has a severe moisture problem. The best time to check a slab for dampness is just after a rainstorm when the ground is saturated with water. To make the test, place 1-foot squares of plastic in half a dozen spots around the floor, carefully taping down all edges. After 24 hours, take up the plastic. Condensation under the plastic indicates that moisture is coming through the concrete. If there is a significant amount of condensation, don't lay the parquet. For only a slight amount of condensation, there are some parquet adhesives on the market that contain a moisture-retardant element; these can be used in cases where there is a minor moisture problem. Laminated parquet should be used in this case. Trowel on a layer of mastic with the flat side of the trowel before applying it with the notched side. Alternatively, you can put down a moisture barrier of polyethylene film with a suitable adhesive. A moisture barrier or a moisture-retardant adhesive should always be used below grade even if there is no indication of a moisture problem. Watch for moisture not only from below but also from other sources—seepage through a wall or dripping from a pipe—that could ruin your new floor.

If you're thinking of installing parquet over a recently cast concrete floor, wait 90 days—ample time for the concrete to cure. Make sure the area is well ventilated, and turn the heat on during the cool season. After the 90 days, do the moisture test described above.

If the concrete floor is dry, use a garage floor cleaner (available at auto parts stores) to remove grease and oil. Use a cold chisel and ball-peen hammer to remove any chunks of concrete and fill depressions with a concrete patching mix. If the floor isn't level, use a leveling compound.

ASK A PRO

CAN I SOLVE A MOISTURE PROBLEM OVER A CONCRETE SUBFLOOR?

Moisture coming from above can be prevented by repairing any plumbing leaks. However, there is no easy way to prevent moisture coming up through the concrete slab. Your only options are to put down a moisture barrier of polyethylene film and then place a new layer of concrete, or to completely revamp the drainage around the house—both complicated and expensive options. If you have a significant moisture problem, your best choice is to install ceramic tile instead of parquet.

LAYING PARQUET

After the subfloor is clean and level, remove any baseboards and shoe moldings. If you're laying the parquet over an existing floor, place a square next to the door and mark where the door needs to be cut to clear the new floor. Allow 1/4 inch additional clearance for interior doors: On exterior doors, allow for the type of weather stripping used and remove the doorway threshold. The door casings must be notched to permit the parquet to slip underneath (page 93).

Once the subfloor is ready, mark the working lines. These will keep the joints straight, even if your walls are not. You can start from the center of the room, or from a wall. Start from the center (below) if the room is badly out of square, or if you'll see both opposite walls at once (such as along the length of a hallway). With this method, you'll usually have to cut squares on all four walls, but it ensures that the cut squares will be visually appealing. If you start from a wall (page 35), you'll only have to cut squares on two adjacent walls; try to do this on the least visible walls. A third way to lay out the floor (a variation of the method starting from the center) using diagonal working lines is shown on page 75. This may be visually pleasing, but it requires angled cuts in squares along all four walls. To install self-stick parquet, lay out the project as shown below and then follow the manufacturer's instructions.

Laying out the floor

TOOLKIT
- Tape measure
- Chalk line
- Carpenter's square

Marking the center line

Begin by measuring the room to find the exact center of two facing walls—A and B (below, left). Snap a chalk line (AB) between the two center points. Find the center of walls C and D and again snap a chalk line (CD). To check that these lines cross at a 90° angle, you can use the 3-4-5 method (below, right): From the center, measure 3' along line AB and 4' down line CD. The diagonal distance between these two points will be exactly 5' if the lines are square. If not—and your measurements are correct—the walls are out of square. Adjust line CD until the diagonal is 5'.

Determine how the squares will look around the borders. If they are about one half-square or larger, they won't look like afterthoughts. Make a dry run with loose parquet tiles down from the center along lines AB and CD. If the last piece is less than half a square, move the center line one half-square to one side, as shown, to give you an adjusted working line. Repeat for line CD.

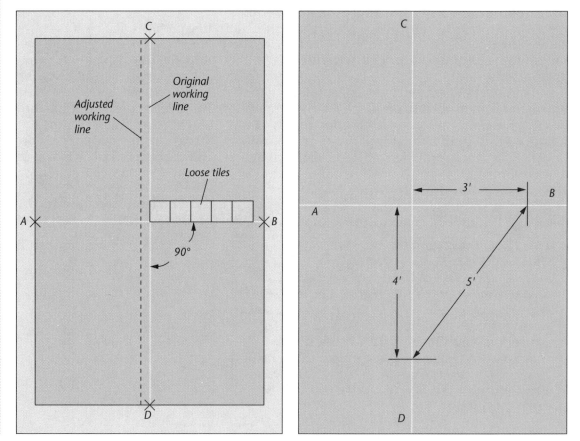

Setting the tile

TOOLKIT
- Putty knife (optional)
- Notched trowel
- Rubber mallet
- Saw
- Hammer
- Floor roller

To finish the floor:
- Drum sander
- Edger

1 ▶ **Spreading the adhesive**
The adhesive, like the wood, should be left at room temperature for 24 hours to warm up. You can also put the can of adhesive in hot water to soften it. You can use a putty knife to transfer some of the adhesive to the floor. Spread the adhesive with the notched trowel held at about a 45° angle. Work the adhesive from several different directions to spread it evenly *(right)*. Be careful not to cover the working lines. Spread only as much as you can comfortably reach and can cover before it starts to dry.

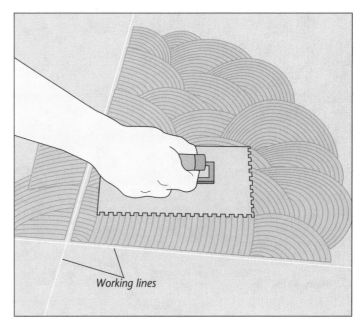

Working lines

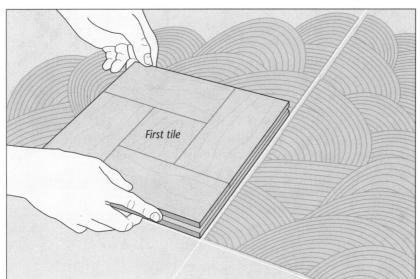

First tile

◀ **2** **Placing the first square**
Place the first square precisely along the intersecting lines. Do this accurately because all remaining tiles will follow this one.

3 ▶ **Laying the next squares**
Lay the second square on the other side of the line as shown at right. Ensure that the squares are against the working lines; match corners exactly and butt the edges together tightly. Do not slide the squares, except for the small amount necessary with tongue-and-groove pieces.

Continue laying the parquet in pyramid fashion *(page 76)*; see page 77 for the diagonal method. Work backward to stay off the parquet for as long as possible. When you must stand on the flooring, put down plywood to distribute your weight.

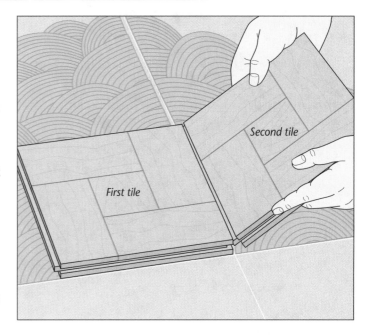

Second tile

First tile

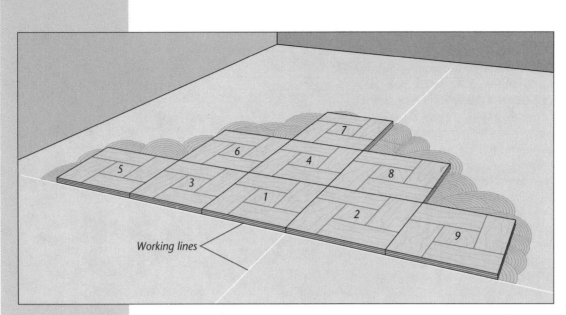

Working lines

4 ▶ **Continuing the pattern across the room**
As you install the parquet, maintain the step pattern and alignment (left). If any adhesive is forced up between the squares or tracked onto the floor surface, wipe it off immediately with a damp cloth. If adhesive dries on the surface, remove it with mineral spirits.

5 ▶ **Bedding the tiles**
As you work, tap the squares with a rubber mallet (right) to bed them and to lower any high corners. To keep the squares from sliding out of position and to prevent adhesive from being forced up between squares while you are walking or kneeling on the newly laid flooring, place plywood over it, as described in step 3.

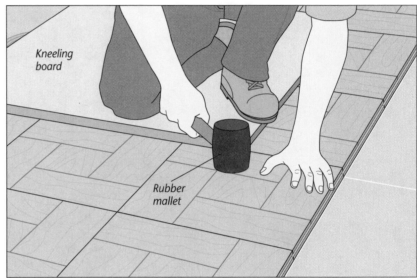

Kneeling board

Rubber mallet

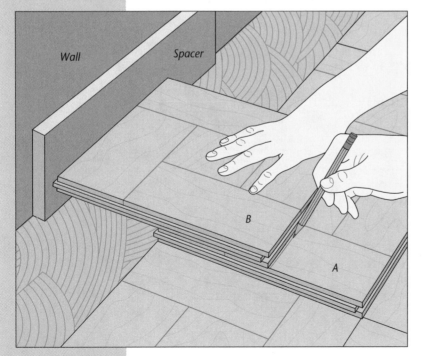

Wall   Spacer

B

A

6 ◀ **Marking the border**
When you reach a wall or other obstacle, you may need to cut squares to fit. Allow for the natural expansion of wood by leaving at least a 1/2" gap between the square and the wall. This gap will be covered by the baseboard or shoe molding. The width of the gap will be determined by the thickness of the parquet; 1/2" parquet will require a 1/2" gap. If the square can't expand, it may buckle. To cut a square (A) to fit, use a piece of scrap wood the same thickness as the parquet as a spacer (left). Set square A on top of the one already in place and set square B against the spacer. Mark the cutting line on square A (left) and cut it.

If your new floor will create a change of level from one room to the next, install a reducer strip—usually a matching piece of wood 1 1/2" wide with a rounded nosing on the outer edge for a finished look. It will fit into the tongues of adjacent squares, or can be butted against exposed grooves.

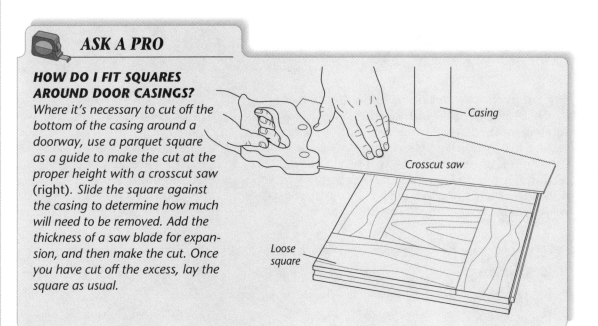

ASK A PRO

HOW DO I FIT SQUARES AROUND DOOR CASINGS?

Where it's necessary to cut off the bottom of the casing around a doorway, use a parquet square as a guide to make the cut at the proper height with a crosscut saw (right). Slide the square against the casing to determine how much will need to be removed. Add the thickness of a saw blade for expansion, and then make the cut. Once you have cut off the excess, lay the square as usual.

Casing

Crosscut saw

Loose square

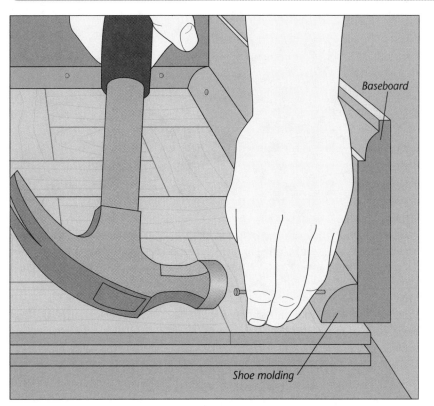

Baseboard

Shoe molding

7 Reinstalling the molding

Nail the baseboard to the wall, followed by the shoe molding *(left)*. Before the adhesive sets, you must roll the parquet to set it and to level any pieces that have popped up. If you've rented the kind of weighted floor roller you fill with water, it should weigh about 150 pounds. The surface of the roller should be smooth and clean. Don't roll prefinished parquet.

8 Finishing

If you've chosen to install unfinished parquet, you'll need to sand and finish it. This is a tricky job and you should consult your flooring supplier for detailed instructions. Here are the basic steps: Seal the room to keep dust out of the rest of the house. The power sanding tools—drum sander and edger—can be rented. Sand the floor on a diagonal with the drum sander, first using a coarse-grit sandpaper and then with medium and fine. Sand the edges of the room with the edger. After sanding, thoroughly vacuum the floor. Apply a stain if desired; the length of time you leave the stain on before wiping off the excess will affect the color. Next, apply a penetrating sealer. (Combined stains and sealers are available.) Finally, apply a coat of wax or a surface finish such as polyurethane.

PARQUET 93

F inishes for parquet floors are either penetrating or surface. To find out which kind you have, try scratching the surface with a coin. If it flakes, it's a surface finish. With a penetrating finish, a good paste wax—not a water-base wax—will give additional protection to the wood. Buff about twice a year; wax about once a year or as needed. Keep in mind that excessive waxing detracts from the floor's appearance.

A parquet floor with a penetrating finish should not be damp-mopped; vacuum and sweep only. Stains can be cleaned with mineral spirits. Clean surface finishes with a damp mop or a mild cleanser, such as white vinegar.

Don't use wax on a surface finish; wax prevents polyurethane from binding, meaning you'll have to strip the floor to apply a new coat. Polyurethane finishes last about three years (less in high-traffic areas).

Replacing a square

TOOLKIT
- Circular saw
- Hammer and butt chisel
- Notched trowel

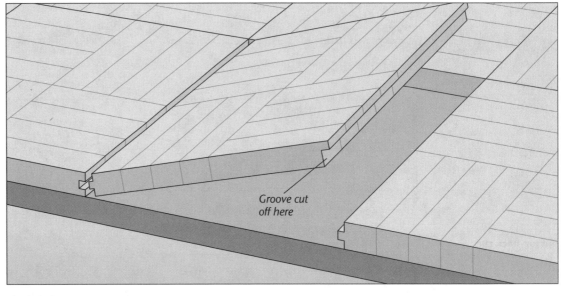

Groove cut off here

Fitting in a new square

For tongue-and-groove parquet, set the blade of a circular saw to the depth of the parquet. Cut around the edges; don't damage adjoining squares. Make some crosscuts in the middle and chisel the tile out. Chip out as much adhesive as you can so the new square will sit flush. To fit the square, cut off the lower edge of the groove. Spread adhesive on the square and slip the tongue into the groove of an existing square (above); press down.

If the square is square-edged, chisel out the old square and adhesive. Use the same adhesive (but not too much) for the new tile; you should be able to fit it without a mallet. Keep off the floor for 24 hours. Wait two to five days and refinish, if necessary.

REPAIRING THE FINISH

If you have a penetrating finish, a small area can be cleaned with mineral spirits and No. 3 steel wool. Wipe off the excess cleanser and, after a few hours, buff and rewax. The entire floor can be renewed using a reconditioning product, after which the floor can be rewaxed.

For a surface finish, first remove any wax with a wax-removal product. If this doesn't work, the floor must be refinished because the new coat won't bond well. If you can remove the wax or if there is none, dull the floor with sandpaper or steel wool and apply a new coat of finish.

For superficial burn marks, lightly sand the affected area; wipe up the sanding residue with a damp cloth. For deeper burns, carefully scrape out the burned wood with a sharp knife. Apply one or more coats of commercial scratch hider, putty stick, or stick shellac.

Shallow scratches can be hidden with one or two applications of scratch hider or crayon. Fill deeper scratches and gouges with matching wood putty, putty stick, or stick shellac. Let the area dry and then sand with fine-grit sandpaper and refinish.

TILE GLOSSARY

Backing
Any material used as a foundation for ceramic tile. Also the underside of a resilient or wood tile.

Backsplash
The wall area covered with ceramic tile behind a sink or counter.

Batten
A wood strip, usually a 1x2 or 1x3, giving a rigid guide to butt ceramic tiles against.

Bedding
Gently tapping a tile so it is set firmly in the adhesive.

Bond
The adherence of a material to another. An effective bond must be made between the tile and adhesive and between the adhesive and backing. Also a pattern of joint alignment, as in jack-on-jack or running bond.

Bullnose tile
A ceramic tile rounded at one edge; used for trim, such as at the top of a wainscot.

Button-back tile
So called because of the bumps on the underside that reduce friction as the tile shrinks in the kiln.

Casing
Trim applied around a door or window.

Cement backerboard
A water-resistant cement sheet product that is installed over plywood subfloors or to wall studs as a backing for ceramic tile.

Cement, portland
A manufactured product, as opposed to natural cement. A basic ingredient in mortar.

Chalk line
A reference line marked on a work surface by snapping a stretched string coated with chalk.

Cove base
A flexible vinyl or rubber trim strip often 4" high, used with resilient flooring instead of baseboards and shoe molding.

Cove tile
A ceramic tile with a curved edge used at the bottom of a wall to join with floor tile.

Curing
The process by which mortar or adhesive sets. Mortar needs to be kept damp ("damp cure"), while most adhesives cure as they dry ("dry cure").

Dry run
Laying tile out on the floor before applying adhesive, to determine the best layout and minimize the number of cut tiles.

Effloresence
A white powdery deposit caused by water dissolving mineral salts in concrete.

Expansion joint
Allows movement between adjoining sections of concrete slabs and helps to prevent cracking due to expansion and contraction.

Extruded tile
A tile that is formed when plastic clay mixtures are forced through a pug mill opening or die, producing a continuous ribbon of formed clay. The proper sizes are created by cutting the clay with a wire cutter.

Field tiles
Regular tiles used on the main surface of a wall or floor, as opposed to specially shaped trim tiles.

Flexible joint
A caulked joint that allows two planes to move independently, such as the joint between a wall and floor. Should be approximately 1/4" wide.

Glaze
A hard, glassy coating fused to the top surface of a ceramic tile by firing at a high temperature.

Grade
Ground level of a house; floors are classified either as above grade, on grade, or below grade.

Grout
Fills the joints between ceramic tiles to keep out dirt and liquids.

Gypsum wallboard
Also known as drywall. Commonly used as a backing for ceramic tile on walls.

Jack-on-jack bond
A pattern of setting tile where all the joints are aligned. This is the traditional bond pattern for bathrooms.

Kickspace
The bottom of a counter which has been recessed for toe space.

Leg
Narrow column of ceramic tiles on the walls in front of a bathtub.

Mastic
A gluelike adhesive used for tile.

Moisture barrier
A layer of a material such as building paper applied to the wall studs to keep moisture out of the wall. Polyethylene sheeting can also be used; this will keep out air as well as moisture.

Mortar
Used in a thick bed to bond outdoor tile to a concrete slab; composed of water, portland cement, and sand (may contain lime). Thin-set adhesives can also be referred to as mortar.

Mosaic
Small ceramic tiles arranged in a pattern and joined into sheets by cotton or paper mesh or by dabs of silicone rubber. Also an intricate pattern made with small ceramic tiles or pieces of ceramic tile, wood, glass, or stone.

Open time
Time during which an adhesive retains its ability to stick to a tile and bond it to a backing.

Parquet
Flooring made up of squares or pieces of wood block.

Paver
Similar to a quarry tile, but molded rather than extruded before being fired.

Pickets
Narrow, pointed tiles used to provide variety in a pattern.

Porcelain tile
The most glasslike, water-resistant tile; made of highly refined clay.

Quarry tile
Tough, water-resistant clay tiles (glazed or unglazed) made by extrusion.

Resilient tile
Floor tile made from solid vinyl, vinyl composition, cork, or rubber.

Running bond
A pattern of setting tile where the joints are staggered. It is similar to the standard brick pattern.

Sealer
A product used to protect tile and grout from water penetration and stains.

Seconds
Tiles with minor defects of glaze, color, or form; usually sold at a substantial discount.

Shim
A thin piece of wood or metal used to make a surface flat or level.

Shoe molding
Typically a quarter-round molding attached to the bottom of the baseboard, covering the joint between the wall and floor.

Shower pan
The bottom of the shower; it comes either prefabricated or the ceramic tile must be professionally installed.

Silicone rubber caulk
A product used to fill joints, such as around a bathtub. Its main properties include its abilities to remain flexible and waterproof, and to resist mildew and extremes of cold and heat.

Spacers
Molded plastic cross-, T-, or Y-shaped pieces used to separate ceramic tile on floors or walls. Small pieces of plywood can be used instead.

Splines
Thin wood, metal, or plastic strips on the underside of a parquet square that hold the individual pieces of wood together.

Striking off
Leveling a sand or mortar bed, or freshly placed concrete, by dragging a board across the top.

Stud
A vertical framing member used in a wall.

Subfloor
The first layer of the floor structure—either plywood or boards fastened to the joists or to a concrete slab.

Thin-set
A cement-base adhesive used for ceramic tile. Available with latex or polymer additives.

Tile stick
Marked with the size of tile and grout joint. Used to keep joints evenly spaced.

Tongue-and-groove tile
A type of parquet square with a tongue on one edge that fits into a corresponding groove on the edge of another square.

Tooling
Compacting a mortar joint using a convex jointer.

Underlayment
Material laid over the subfloor used to smooth irregularities and increase rigidity; used as a backing for tile. Must be appropriate material for type of tile to be installed.

Vitreous
Having the quality of glass; a characteristic of porcelain tile (a type of ceramic tile).

Wainscot
A facing, such as ceramic tile, resilient tile, or parquet that ends part of the way up a wall.

Waterproof membrane
A means of waterproofing which is applied over wallboard or cement backerboard. The membrane is made of fiberglass mesh and liquid rubber.

Wet saw
A special power saw for cutting ceramic tile, with a built-in water-cooling system.

Working lines
Lines laid out on the subfloor, underlayment, or wall to keep the first tile courses straight and to adjust for any crookedness in walls or floors.

INDEX